Penguin Books
Penguin Skills Series

**Penguin Advanced
Writing Skills**

Penguin Skills Series

Penguin Advanced Writing Skills

James O'Driscoll

Penguin Books

PENGUIN BOOKS

Published by the Penguin Group
27 Wrights Lane, London W8 5TZ, England
Viking Penguin Inc., 40 West 23rd Street, New York, New York 10010, USA
Penguin Books Australia Ltd, Ringwood, Victoria, Australia
Penguin Books Canada Ltd, 2801 John Street, Markham, Ontario, Canada L3R 1B4
Penguin Books (NZ) Ltd, 182–190 Wairau Road, Auckland 10, New Zealand

Penguin Books Ltd, Registered Offices: Harmondsworth, Middlesex, England

First published 1984
10 9 8 7 6 5 4 3 2

Copyright © James O'Driscoll, 1984
All rights reserved

Made and printed in Great Britain by
Hazell Watson & Viney Limited
Member of BPCC plc
Aylesbury, Bucks, England
Set in VIP Palatino and VIP Helvetica

Except in the United States of America, this book is sold subject
to the condition that it shall not, by way of trade or otherwise, be lent,
re-sold, hired out, or otherwise circulated without the
publisher's prior consent in any form of binding or cover other than
that in which it is published and without a similar condition
including this condition being imposed on the subsequent purchaser

Contents

To the student		8
Notes		10
To the teacher		11

Unit	Areas of focus	
1 Writing about an incident I *Squirrel*	Describing decisions Connecting past events	16
2 Writing about an incident II *A brush with the law*	Giving the background to a story Explaining why things happened	23
3 Writing about an incident III *A brush with the law*	Showing your attitude Commenting on events	29
4 Writing letters of protest *Sir!*	Being ironic Anticipating objections to your argument	36
5 Writing about an incident IV *Earthquake*	Describing feelings and impressions Connecting past events	42
6 News reporting *Disaster*	Moving from general to particular Summarizing	49
7 Academic essay/report – process *Elections*	Using and explaining specialist terms Impersonal verbal constructions	55
8 Academic essay/report – narrative *The end of the Saxon kings*	Sequencing Connecting past events	62
9 Writing information in tabular form	Timetables and schedules Flow diagrams	72

Contents

10	Writing advertisements *Classified*	Abbreviating Careful description	79
11	Writing letters of request *Looking for work*	Aspects of letters of request Layout and conventions of letter writing	85
12	Tabulating biographical information *Curriculum vitae*	Special language Organizing tabulated information	91
13	Describing people *Charles Dickens*	Degrees of probability Point of view	97
14	More letters of request *Problems*	Different levels of request	105
15	Letters of reply *With regard to . . .*	Agreeing to and refusing requests Explaining and reassuring	111
16	Letters of information and advice *Britain*	Informal advice Formal advice	117
17	Discussing a phenomenon I *The problem of violence in cities*	Defining the scope of an essay Analysing opinions	123
18	Discussing a phenomenon II *The problem of violence in cities*	Amplifying your argument Pointing the way	130
19	Discussing a phenomenon III *The problem of violence in cities*	Exemplifying your argument Pointing the way	137

20 Discussing a phenomenon *The instinct for collecting things*	IV Using an informal tone Illustrating your statements	145

Key   151

To the student

As an advanced learner of English you can easily write correct sentences, but perhaps you have difficulty organizing your ideas when you have to write something longer. Perhaps you get annoyed because you cannot effectively express what you mean. If you ever write to people in English, you probably find that sometimes they do not completely understand you; or perhaps they think the way you express yourself is a little strange. The aim of this book is to help you get over difficulties like these. If you are going to take an examination in English it will help you to pass it.

The book gives you examples of the major types of writing. It teaches you to write well by concentrating on certain aspects of each type. For example, writing a narrative means that you have to connect a large number of past events which may differ in their relationship to each other. There are several sections in the book on *Connecting past events*.

In the book there are units on writing stories, letters, descriptions, and opinions. There are also units on more specialized types of writing, such as reports for a newspaper, or the kind of writing you need to do if you are studying a subject in English.

Each unit begins with a text. The first thing you will be asked to do is the *Reading practice*. This provides you with an interesting and useful way of approaching the text. When you are doing this exercise it is important not to worry about complete understanding of it. Going slowly through every line is very boring.

The *Reading practice* is usually followed immediately by the *Textwork*. Here you will have an opportunity to read the text again, this time in more detail. The *Understanding* exercise is there to make sure that you understand everything from the text that you need to understand. The *Vocabulary* exercise draws your attention to some words and phrases that you might find useful.

If, after this, there are still some things in the text that you feel you do not understand, it does not matter. The text is only there as an example of the type of writing to be practised in this unit. The real aim of the book is to improve your *writing*.

The textwork is followed by *Areas of focus*. These are the most important part of each unit. In them you learn about and practise a particular aspect of writing, of which there are examples in the text.

Each area of focus is divided into two sections. There is the *Study* section, which usually asks you to look back at the text and identify examples. It gives you useful phrases, with definitions of their functions. Then there is the *Practice* section. This gives you

To the student

the opportunity to try out what you have just learnt. Sometimes you have to write down single sentences. Sometimes you are asked to write longer, connected pieces. In these, you should imagine that what you are writing is actually part of a complete piece of writing.

The practice exercises in the areas of focus are controlled; if you cannot do them you know that you need to look again at the *Study* section. But the *Extended writing*, which follows immediately afterwards, gives you the chance for a much freer range of expression. Here you will be asked to write complete texts yourself. Normally, when the writing is not for a specific purpose, there is no instruction to write a particular number of words. In these cases, follow the advice of your teacher, or train yourself to write the number of words required in whatever examination you intend to sit.

At the back of the book there is a key to some of the exercises so that you can check your answers. Explanations are sometimes provided. Do not worry if you look for the answers to an exercise in the key and they are not there. This means either that the exercise is self checking (you will not be able to continue until you have understood, so look again!), or that the answer is unimportant; the doing of the exercise is the important thing. Sometimes only the first few answers for an exercise are given. They are there to give you the general idea if you are having difficulty.

Two final points: if you are a student working on your own, you will find it useful to have a dictionary near you while you are working through the book. Secondly, please read the *Notes* on the next page carefully. They will help you work through the book more effectively.

Good luck and good writing!

Notes

1 The numbers at the sides of the texts refer to paragraphs, *not* to lines.
2 The abbreviation 'para.' is sometimes used for paragraph.
3 The items in the *Vocabulary* exercises are in the same order as they appear in the text.
4 In the *Vocabulary* exercises:
a a stroke (/) means that an alternative or equivalent meaning follows immediately afterwards. For example:
   shock/terror
means that the word you are looking for could mean both of these things.
b a comma is followed by extra information on the use or exact meaning of the word you are looking for.
c (round brackets) give a syntactic context. For example
   move (across something) with difficulty
means that the word you are looking for is usually found with the word 'across' after it.
5 Some matching exercises in the *Study* section of the *Areas of focus* may have to be done by a process of elimination.
6 [Square brackets] round a word or phrase show that what is inside them is an example of the *kind* of phrase that could fit here. This is particularly important with verbs, where [DO] stands for any verb. Thus [HAD DONE] means the past perfect tense of any verb, [BE DOING] means the present continuous tense of any verb, and so on.
7 (Round brackets) around part of a phrase mean that this part is optional. It is sometimes omitted.

To the teacher

Who the book is for

1 It is best suited to Higher Intermediate/Advanced level learners: for example, to those about halfway between Cambridge FCE and CPE, or to those graded in a GCE English Language exam year. It could certainly be used at a higher level, in fact at a near native-speaker level of ability, where specific practice in written skills was required. It could be used at a slightly lower level of general language ability, but in this case there is a danger that the vocabulary load and length of texts would slow things down too much to provide effective writing practice.
2 It is not designed for any specific examination, but since it involves essay-writing of various types, letter-writing, and a number of other forms of writing for specific purposes, it could quite comfortably be used by a student preparing for the Cambridge CPE, RSA Stage 3, JMB, GCE English Language or any other similar examination.
3 It is designed for older teenagers and adults.

What the book covers

1 It concentrates on writing as a separate skill and therefore does *not* contain material for two distinct types of writing. These are:
written material which is to be spoken (e.g. dialogues);
very informal writing (e.g. letters to close friends).
2 Otherwise it aims to cover and teach all types of writing that an educated native speaker would expect to be competent in and that are not over-specialized. Obviously, limits of space mean that examples of writing for every situation cannot be given. Teachers with more specific purposes may like to note that it does not contain examples of business reports, public notices, press statements, memoranda, telex, form-filling, or longer texts such as brochures, owners' manuals or sets of regulations. However, a study of the areas of focus on the Contents page will show that it draws attention to and practises most of the language characteristics of these forms.

What the book teaches

1 It identifies specific features of language use which are characteristic of certain types of writing (e.g. connecting past

To the teacher

events, anticipating objections to your argument), draws the student's attention to them, and practises them in a comparatively controlled form before suggesting their use in a wider context.
2 To the extent that it gives examples of:

   narrative essays/articles of different emotional tone
   argumentative essays of different emotional tone
   academic essays of narrative and explanatory type
   letters to newspapers and prospective employers
   other letters of request and reply
   newspaper reports
   classified advertisements *and*
   various tabular forms of presentation,

it also teaches by example other features which are not specifically practised.
3 Since teaching any kind of language production involves the study of a model, the book will inevitably cause some improvement in reading skills and acquisition of passive vocabulary. Teachers may sometimes wish to slow the pace down and emphasize these aspects more. However, the danger of slowing the pace down so much that the main aim of the book – the improvement of *writing* skills – is lost sight of should not be ignored.

How the book progresses

1 It is intended to be worked through from beginning to end. This is not so much because there is any grading in the linguistic content, but because the conceptual content gradually becomes more sophisticated, and because the same thematic material is often reworked as a way of cutting down on vocabulary and reading input, so that attention is more easily focused on production.
2 Units 1–9 and 12–13 are basically narration/description.
Units 10–11 and 14–16 are basically suasion.
Units 17–20 are basically argument/discussion.
However, these overall skills are by no means exclusive of each other. A glance at the *Areas of focus* will show that Units 3 and 4 focus on attitudinal language, as does Unit 13, and that Unit 10 obviously involves description.

To the teacher

3 As far as writing format is concerned
a Units 1–3, 5, 7–8, 13 and 17–20 are of the essay/article type. However, there is much variation within this type. Units 1–3, 5 and 20 are of the straightforward journalism/language exam type, while Units 7–8 are clearly of the academic type. Units 13 and 17–19 could be either.
b Units 11 and 14–16 involve writing letters for specific purposes.
c The other units are of particular types. They are
Unit 4 – letter to a newspaper
Unit 6 – newspaper reporting
Unit 9 – diagrammatic presentation of information for academic purposes
Unit 10 – classified advertisements for a newspaper
Unit 12 – tabulated personal information.
4 There is much variation of tone within the types and formats. Units 1 and 20, for example, are informal and humorous, while Units 17–19 are dry and serious.
5 A study of the *Areas of focus* in the Contents will show an overall progression, although it is certainly not linear, from the more straightforward to the more sophisticated. Units 1–2, 5 and 8 focus on the effective presentation of narrative information. Units 3 and 4 introduce attitude and opinion at a syntactic level. Unit 6 focuses on the organization of narrative information at a textual level. Units 7 and 10 return to the syntactic level of language but this time in a more specific context. Units 9 and 11 focus again on organization at a textual level, also in a specific context. Unit 12 involves both the syntactic and textual levels, again in a specific context. Unit 13 reintroduces attitudinal language, but at a more sophisticated level. Units 14–16 focus on effective suasion. Units 17–19 concentrate on the effective presentation of argument. Unit 20 does this also, but it has the added element of a particularly coloured tone.

What each Unit contains

Reading practice – based on all or a previewed part of the text

The text itself

Textwork – divided into
a Understanding
b Vocabulary

To the teacher

Two *Areas of focus* – each divided into
a Study
b Practice

Extended writing – divided into
a loosely guided
b completely free.

Every unit contains these features in the order listed above, with the following exceptions:
In Units 1 and 8 one of the *Areas of focus* comes before the *Textwork*.
Unit 2 has an extra, summarizing, category under the *Textwork* and no completely free stage in the *Extended writing*.
Unit 9 has no text or *Textwork* as such.
Unit 14 has only one *Area of focus*.

Using the book

1 The *Reading practice* is intended mainly as an interesting approach to the text. However, it often introduces an aspect which is going to be concentrated on later in the unit.
2 The *Textwork* is intended as an opportunity for fuller understanding and slower reading of the text than the *Reading practice* allows. Even so, detailed questioning is avoided.
a In some cases the *Understanding* section may lead students to aspects which are to be focused on later. Although interest in the passage can always be exploited, the main aim is to stay on the text just long enough for students to feel confident, without getting bogged down in 'text crawling'.
b The *Vocabulary* section is intended partly to head off such tendencies. In addition, students may have an opportunity to use some of the vocabulary items, since the practice stages later in the unit often exploit the same thematic material.
3 The *Areas of focus* are the meat of the unit.
a The *Study* section is intended to be just that. It often starts with a comment that the teacher may wish to expand or ignore altogether. The usual procedure is that questions of a very specific and leading nature identify the area of focus. Then there is usually a presentation of the focus in summarized form and/or a matching, multiple choice or similar exercise to help the student get the feel of the item in focus.
b In the *Practice* section students are asked to use the language

To the teacher

they have just studied, in a controlled format at first. When going through this section in class, ample time should be allowed for each item. Many require some thought and invention. This is a writing, not oral, skills book, and it is recommended that students should be given time to write their answers down before class checking takes place. Many of the exercises can be done by discussion in groups.
4   The *Extended writing* sections require students to be able to integrate the language they have focused on, by writing something of nearly the same length as the text.
a The first exercise in the *Extended writing* section is guided, in the sense that content notes are provided. As a result, when a post-mortem on the students' performance is held, attention still tends to be on the areas of focus. This exercise often stimulates very good groupwork.
b The second exercise is normally straightforward, unguided work.

Timing

Potentially, all of the work could be done by the students outside class time, which would then be used simply for checking. Conversely, everything could be done in class. Thus the book could take anything from twenty-five to 125 contact hours to work through.

In practice, a happy medium is likely to prevail. With a class of about twenty students, where everything is done in class except the second part of the *Extended writing*, each unit will take from three to five hours to work through (depending on its length, its difficulty, the ability of the students and the style of the teacher), and around eighty contact hours should be allowed for the whole book. This time would be slightly reduced if the *Reading practice* were normally prepared outside class and greatly reduced if the *Textwork* were also prepared outside class.

In any circumstance where there is pressure of time, the *Reading practice* and *Textwork* should be hurried, but *not* the *Areas of focus*.

PLEASE READ THE NOTES ON p. 10

Unit 1
Writing about an incident I
Squirrel

Reading practice
The paragraphs below are taken from a story. As they appear here, they are in the wrong order. One of them is the first paragraph of the story. The remaining paragraphs form part of the rest of the story.
1 Read them and, as fast as you can, decide which is the first paragraph.
2 Read them again. In what order do you think the remaining paragraphs appear in the complete story?

1   Eventually, my wife found a ladder and I got out that way. Of course, I had to go to hospital, where I was given a couple of stitches and told they would have to keep me there for forty-eight hours under observation in case there was any delayed concussion. No wedding.

2   This we did, and everything went smoothly until I tried to get out of the backyard myself. Then the horrible realization hit me. Just as Squirrel could get down to this yard on his own but not out of it, so I was now trapped.

3   It was Easter Sunday and the next day we were going to an island to be guests at a wedding. A friend of ours was staying with us because she was coming too. She was the first person up that morning. When she went into the kitchen to make some coffee, she felt hot, so she opened the back door. That was the beginning of the disaster.

4   However, because it was Easter Sunday, nobody in this building was at home. We had to get Squirrel back immediately because we were leaving the next day. There was no alternative but to scamper along the tops of the walls of a number of backyards until we arrived at *the* backyard. Then I could jump down and hand Squirrel up to my wife on the top of the wall.

What made you decide on the order?
What do you think the story is about? (Try to guess. It does not matter if you turn out to be wrong. The important thing is to use all the evidence.)

Describing decisions

Study
How did you know that paragraph 4 of the text above is not the last paragraph of the whole story?
Things do not always happen by themselves. Sometimes they happen because you thought about the situation and decided what to do. In these cases you can add variety and interest to your story by describing your decisions rather than the event itself.

Unit 1

Read paragraph 4 again and decide
• which sentences state the situation/the problem;
• which sentences describe the response to the problem.
Now underline the verb patterns used to show what the writer decided to do. There are two of them.
Here is a list of phrases which can go with these verb patterns:
(I thought) I could . . .
(I decided) There was no alternative but to . . .
The only thing to do was to . . .
There was nothing left to do but to . . .
All I could do was to . . .
Can you think of any other phrases which would fit in this kind of situation? What about 'I decided to . . .'?

Practice
1 The sentences below state certain problem-situations. A solution, or solutions, is given for each situation. With each one, choose from the 'decision' phrases above to write the solution to the problem. (In some cases you may need to write more than one sentence.)
a When I finally arrived in Florence it was eleven o'clock at night and all the hotels were full.
(Solution: find a café – stay there the night)
b Suddenly I slipped and fell right into the river. There were lots of people watching and I felt very stupid.
(Solution: pretend I had done it on purpose – swim to the other side)
c I had to get home quickly, but the whole city was covered with several centimetres of water and there were no buses or trains running . . .
(Solution: taxi)
. . . but there were not any taxis either.
(Solution: walk)
d I needed the phone number immediately. But it was in my wallet and I had left *that* in the local shop, which had closed several hours before.
(Solution: ring doorbells nearby – find out the shopkeeper's home number – phone him)
e I had dropped one of my earrings down the drain in the bathroom. I tried fishing for it with a coat hanger, but it was no good, as I couldn't see anything.
(Solution: get the vacuum cleaner – suck everything up – empty out the dustbag)

17

f I was trapped in the basement. There was no way out and the water level was rising fast.
(Solution: hope for a miracle)

2 In each of the following situations continue the story by writing *at least* one sentence in which you describe what decisions you took.
a We had decided to stay in and watch TV but we couldn't decide on a choice of programme. I wanted to see 'Sportsview' and she preferred something on the other channel.
b I felt extremely hungry but there was no food in the house and all the shops were shut.
c It was a very hot day and there was no one around. I took off all my clothes and plunged into the cool waters of the lake. I stayed in for about ten minutes, loving every minute of it. But when I got out, my clothes were nowhere to be found. Someone had stolen them.
d I was just about to ask for the bill when I remembered I had no money on me at all.
e My cousin from Canada was a bit difficult to entertain. We had decided to go out that night but she didn't like the cinema or the theatre and she was on a diet.
f What was I to do? It wasn't much fun standing outside my house at two in the morning in the freezing cold without my keys.

Textwork

Understanding
First check that you know these words:
backyard   window-sill   concrete
corrugated   concussion
Now read the whole of the story about Squirrel and answer the questions which follow it.

1   It was Easter Sunday, and the next day we were going to an island to be guests at a wedding. A friend of ours was staying with us because she was coming too. She was the first person up that morning. When she went into the kitchen to make some coffee, she felt hot, so she opened the back door. That was the beginning of the disaster.
2   At that time we had a young and rather stupid cat who had a flair for getting trapped in a nearby backyard. He could get down into this place

but, once there, he couldn't jump high enough to get out. Well, as soon as Elena, our friend, opened the back door, out shot the cat and it wasn't long before we could hear the familiar plaintive whines which meant he was trapped in the usual place.

The usual process of retrieving Squirrel (that was the cat's name) was straightforward, although rather embarrassing. We simply went round and knocked on somebody's door in the block of flats which gave access to this particular backyard.

However, because it was Easter Sunday, nobody in this building was at home. We had to get Squirrel back immediately because we were leaving the next day. There was no alternative but to scamper along the tops of the walls of a number of backyards until we arrived at *the* backyard. Then I could jump down and hand Squirrel up to my wife on the top of the wall.

This we did, and everything went smoothly until I tried to get out of the backyard myself. Then the horrible realization hit me. Just as Squirrel could get down to this yard on his own but not out of it, so I was now trapped.

Restraining myself from making Squirrel-like whines, I looked around for a way out. On one side of the yard there was a window-sill and, just above it, a piece of corrugated plastic coming out from the wall. It must have been there to take the rainwater away from some steps which were directly underneath it and led down to a cellar.

I thought that if I got on to the window-sill I could then scramble across the corrugated plastic on to the top of the wall. I would only need to put one foot on the plastic to do it. But as soon as I put my weight on it, the whole thing gave way as its wooden supports were torn out of the wall and wood, plastic and myself went crashing down on to the steps ten feet below.

Having bumped in an undignified manner down all the steps, I hit my head hard on a concrete wall next to the cellar door. Blood started spurting from it as I picked myself up and shook myself, wondering what had happened. My wife looked on in horror. And I was still stuck in the backyard.

The irony was that no sooner had all this happened than my wife found a ladder and I got out that way. Of course, I had to go to hospital, where I was given a couple of stitches and told they would have to keep me there for forty-eight hours under observation in case there was any delayed concussion. No wedding.

At the hospital they asked me what had happened. A road accident? Somebody had attacked me? 'Well, I was rescuing this cat, you see, and . . .'

What was the usual way of getting Squirrel back when he was trapped?
Why was it difficult this time?
Did the writer and his wife carry out their plan successfully?

Unit 1

What went wrong?
How did the writer hurt his head?
Why wasn't his plan to get out of the yard successful?
Why did the writer have to stay in hospital for two days?
Why was this particularly annoying?
How do you think the writer felt when he tried to explain to the hospital staff how the accident had happened?
Apart from paragraph 4, can you find any other examples of 'describing decisions' in the text?

Vocabulary
1 Explain the meaning of these phrases as they appear in the text:
   the horrible realization hit me
   Restraining myself from . . . Squirrel-like whines
   Having bumped in an undignified manner
   I picked myself up
   in case there was any delayed concussion
2 Now find the words or phrases in the text which mean:
   a talent
   went out immediately and very quickly
   fetching/getting back
   was the way to enter
   move (across something) with difficulty
   collapsed
   coming out with great force

Connecting past events

Study
1 Below are some important events which happened in one part of the story. Find the relevant part of the text and fill in the missing events.
   I put my weight on the corrugated plastic / . . . / Its wooden supports were torn out of the wall / . . . / I bumped down all the steps / . . . / I hit my head on the concrete wall / . . . / Blood started spurting from it / . . . / All this happened / . . . / I got out that way.
2 You now have a list of eleven events. Look carefully at the parts of the text where they occur. You will notice that they are all fitted into only four sentences. Study how the events within each sentence are connected.
3 Some of the events are connected because they happened

simultaneously (at exactly the same time). In these cases the writer used the pattern
[DID] as [DID]
(See the notes on page 10 for the explanation of the [brackets].)
4 Some of the events are connected because they happened *instantaneously* (very quickly one after the other). In these cases the writer used three patterns. They are:
[DID] and [DID]
as soon as [DID], [DID]
no sooner [HAD DONE] than [DID]
Here are two more:
when [DID], [DID]
the second [DID], [DID]
To understand the difference in meaning between these patterns, try substituting one for the other with the same details. Does it change the meaning at all? If so, how? (There are also some examples in other parts of the text which might help you.)

Practice
Now use the verb patterns to connect these sentences:
1 I patted the dog. It bit me.
2 I put down the receiver. The phone started ringing again.
3 John fired the gun. Jack hit the ground like a sack of potatoes.
4 I rang the bell. The door was opened by a short middle-aged man. I went inside.
5 I rang the bell. The door creaked open by itself.
6 I opened the door. The full force of the hurricane hit me.
7 (It was a very unlucky year for California.) The floodwaters abated. An earthquake hit the area.
8 The result of the election was beyond doubt. People started celebrating in the streets.
9 They realized they weren't welcome. They left.
10 He passed through customs. He phoned his girlfriend. She came to meet him.

Extended writing

1 Below is a short story in note form. Make it into a short essay. Use the phrases and verb patterns you have dealt with in this unit *where appropriate* (it is not usually a good idea to over-use a particular language pattern). Use paragraphs!

Unit 1

weekend in London with friends
important meeting in Oxford early Monday
late Sunday night
February
very cold, rain, biting wind
got out of London
windscreen wipers stopped working
drove with one arm out of window
wiped windscreen with cloth
worked quite well
got to crossroads
only one car on main road
in distance – get across easily
middle of main road
engine stalled
other car much nearer than I had thought
couldn't stop
hit me
knew I was going to be all right
spun round on impact
whole windscreen came out
went sailing across road
got out of car
talked to other driver
other cars went speeding past
. . .
started off again
realized how useful a windscreen is
freezing
no garage nearby, no phone nearby
couldn't leave car
kept driving . . .

2 Write an essay about *one* of the following:
a A terrible mistake and its consequences.
b A road accident.
c A very embarrassing situation.

Unit 2
Writing about an incident II
A brush with the law

Reading practice
1 You are going to read a narrative essay. Look at the title above and try to guess what the story is about.
2 The first paragraph of the essay is printed below. Read it and see if it makes you change your opinion about the contents of the story and what details it is going to give.

I have only once been in trouble with the law. The whole process of being arrested and taken to court was a rather unpleasant experience at the time, but it makes a good story now. What makes it rather disturbing was the arbitrary circumstances both of my arrest and my subsequent fate in court.

What is the writer's attitude to his story going to be? Angry? Sad? Amused? Serious? (Perhaps it is more than just one of these!)

Textwork

Understanding
First check that you know these words and phrases:
loitering   the sixties'   'youth counterculture'
disreputable   *au fait*   Magistrates' Court
Cultural note: In Britain, milk is delivered to houses in bottles every morning.
Now read the passage carefully and answer the questions which follow it.

  I have only once been in trouble with the law. The whole process of being arrested and taken to court was a rather unpleasant experience at the time, but it makes a good story now. What makes it rather disturbing was the arbitrary circumstances both of my arrest and my subsequent fate in court.
  It happened in February about twelve years ago. I had left school a couple of months before that and was not due to go to university until the following October. I was still living at home at the time.
  One morning I was in Richmond, a suburb of London near where I lived. I was looking for a temporary job so that I could save up some money to go travelling. As it was a fine day and I was in no hurry, I was taking my time, looking in shop windows, strolling in the park, and sometimes just stopping and looking around me. It must have been this obvious aimlessness which led to my downfall.
  It was about half past eleven when it happened. I was just walking out of the local library, having unsuccessfully sought employment there, when I

23

Unit 2

saw a man walking across the road with the obvious intention of talking to me. I thought he was going to ask me the time. Instead, he said he was a police officer and he was arresting me. At first I thought it was some kind of joke. But then another policeman appeared, this time in uniform, and I was left in no doubt.

5   'But what for?' I asked.
'Loitering with intent to commit an arrestable offence,' he said.
'What offence?' I asked.
'Theft,' he said.
'Theft of what?' I asked.
'Milk bottles,' he said, and with a perfectly straight face too!
'Oh,' I said.

6   It turned out there had been a spate of petty thefts in the area, particularly that of stealing milk bottles from doorsteps.

7   Then I made my big mistake. At the time I was nineteen, had long untidy hair, and regarded myself as part of the sixties' 'youth counterculture'. As a result, I wanted to appear cool and unconcerned by the incident so I said, 'How long have you been following me?' in the most casual and conversational tone I could manage. I thus appeared to them to be quite familiar with this sort of situation, and it confirmed them in their belief that I was a thoroughly disreputable character.

8   A few minutes later a police car arrived.
'Get in the back,' they said. 'Put your hands on the back of the front seat and don't move them.'
They got in on either side of me. It wasn't funny any more.

9   At the police station they questioned me for several hours. I continued to try to look worldly and *au fait* with the situation. When they asked me what I had been doing I told them I'd been looking for a job. 'Aha,' I could see them thinking, 'unemployed.'

10   Eventually I was officially charged and told to report to Richmond Magistrates' Court the following Monday. Then they let me go.

Why did the writer go to Richmond?
Would you describe him as unemployed at the time?
Was he surprised to be arrested?
Why exactly did the policeman arrest him?
What does the writer mean by his 'big mistake'?
Do you think this is the end of the story? Why (not)?

Vocabulary

1 Explain the meaning of these phrases as they appear in the text:
the arbitrary circumstances . . . my arrest
this obvious aimlessness
I was left in no doubt

a spate of petty thefts
I was officially charged

2 Now find the words or phrases in the text which mean:
what happened to me afterwards
walking slowly and without purpose, for pleasure
looked for/asked for
made them sure about their opinion
extremely/definitely (para. 7)

Remember that the phrases you are looking for appear in the text in the same order as they are paraphrased here.

Summarizing
Now summarize the story (only!) in sixty words *or less*. Include as much as you can of what happened; the events – but not anything else.

When you have finished your summary, *keep it!* You will need it later.

Probably, you managed to get all, or nearly all, of the narrative detail into sixty words (*if* you are good at summarizing!). And yet the text is more than six times that length. This is because it has a lot of other kinds of information apart from the basic storyline. Now, and in the following unit, we are going to look more closely at some of these aspects of writing.

Giving the background to a story

Study
Stories do not happen in a vacuum. They happen at a particular time and place and they involve particular people. Writers usually include this background information because it makes the story more interesting.

Find the two paragraphs from the text which tell you about the writer's *situation* at the time of the story. There are *no events* in these paragraphs.

Study closely all the verb phrases used in them.

Practice
1 Find the correct form of the verb for each of the verbs in brackets in the following story. The form you use may be any one of the following:

Unit 2

WAS [DOING]   HAD (BEEN) [DONE]
WAS [DONE]   HAD BEEN [DOING]
WAS DUE TO [DO]

Remember that in this list the verb DO stands for any verb.

I glanced nervously at the customs officers through the glass doors. We (land) some time ago and now I (wait) for my luggage. We (wait) for half an hour already and I (get) impatient. Also I was nervous because I (break) the law. One of my bags (cram) with bottles of perfume. I (go) home for Christmas, and a month before I (ask) my four sisters and my mother what they wanted. All of them (say) perfume and I didn't want to disappoint any of them. Another reason for my unease was that if I had any trouble I would miss my train connection, which (leave) in only forty-five minutes.

After another five minutes my luggage appeared and I made ready to go through customs. My apprehension was heightened by the fact that the very last time I (travel) I (stop) and (ask) to open my suitcase.

2   Now write the beginning of a story of a visit to the dentist. You want to set the scene for the story. Make any changes and additions you like and use any verb forms you think are suitable, but you must include all the facts in the order they appear in note form here:

dentist's waiting room
tooth hurt a lot
other appointment arranged a week before for following day
cancel (extra work)
a few days later, tooth even worse
teeth in terrible condition generally
not go for several years
what would dentist say about leaving it so long?

Explaining why things happened

Study
In the first unit you learnt how to describe people's decisions. Sometimes it is more suitable to describe *why* people did things. Answer these questions about the text in this unit:
Why was the writer taking his time in Richmond?
Apart from his appearance, what other reason made the police think that the writer might be going to steal milk bottles?

Why did the police think that the writer was familiar with the situation of being arrested?
Why did the writer say 'How long have you been following me?' and why did he say it in such a casual way?
Why did he want to appear cool and unconcerned by the incident?
You were able to answer these questions because there are certain phrases in the text which link an event (such as those contained in the questions above) with the explanation for it (such as the answers to those questions).
They are:
   AS   IT TURNED OUT   THUS   SO   AS A RESULT
Study their use in the text and decide which phrases appear just before
a the explanation/reason
b the result/consequence
Make two columns.
Here are some more ways of linking cause *a* and effect *b*. Put them in the correct columns.
   BECAUSE   IN THIS WAY   CONSEQUENTLY

Practice
1 Use the phrases you have just studied to make the following groups of sentences into coherent pieces of writing (but *not necessarily* into one sentence).
a There was a large demonstration going on in the centre of town. I got held up in a traffic jam for more than an hour. I was extremely late for my appointment.
b I got held up in a traffic jam for more than an hour. I was late for my appointment. There had been a large demonstration in the centre of town.
c I saw two people standing and talking in the middle of the room. I walked up and introduced myself to the person I thought was the Director. He was just another employee. The Director was the other one. Our first meeting got off to a bad start. We still didn't get on well.
d I had introduced myself to the wrong person. Our first meeting got off to a bad start.
e The orange trees had been badly damaged by frost in May. There was a shortage of oranges in the shops. The price was double that of the previous year.
f I couldn't understand why the price of oranges was so high. The

Unit 2

orange trees had been badly damaged by frost in May. There was a shortage of oranges.
2   Now here is a list of jumbled facts. Sort them out into a suitable order and use them in a paragraph, making any changes and additions you feel are desirable.
virtually penniless by Thursday – didn't do any shopping on Tuesday – had to eat out that day – had forgotten that Wednesday was a holiday – had no food in the house at all.
(*Note*: penniless = without money)

Extended writing

Use the language you have practised in this unit (only where appropriate of course!) to write the beginning of a story about a birthday party which you (or someone else) went to.

The story begins as you (or the hero of your story) stand outside the front door. The friend whose birthday it was is a member of the opposite sex. At this time you were rather anxious to impress him/her, so you took a present. However, you were not quite sure about its suitability (you couldn't find what you really wanted to get). Also you wore new clothes which you did not really feel comfortable in.

Write at least 200 words.

Unit 3
Writing about an incident III
A brush with the law continued

Reading practice
The final part of the story from the last unit is printed below. At the moment it is not divided into paragraphs. Read it and decide where the beginnings and ends of *four* paragraphs should occur. (In this case *only*, the numbers at the side refer to *lines* and not to paragraphs.)

I wanted to conduct my own defence in court, but as soon as my father found out what had happened, he hired a very good solicitor. We went along that Monday armed with all kinds of witnesses, including my English teacher from school as a character witness. But he was never
5 called on to give evidence. My 'trial' didn't get that far. The magistrate dismissed the case after fifteen minutes. I was free. The poor police had never stood a chance. The solicitor even succeeded in getting costs awarded against the police. And so I do not have a criminal record. But what was most shocking at the time was the things my acquittal so clearly
10 depended on. I had the 'right' accent, respectable middle-class parents in court, reliable witnesses, and I could obviously afford a very good solicitor. Given the nebulous nature of the charge, I feel sure that if I had come from a different background, and had really been unemployed, there is every chance that I would have been found guilty. While asking for costs
15 to be awarded, my solicitor's case quite blatantly revolved around the fact that I had a 'brilliant academic record'. Meanwhile, just outside the courtroom, one of the policemen who had arrested me was gloomily complaining to my mother that another youngster had been turned against the police. 'You could have been a bit more helpful when we arrested
20 you,' he said to me reproachfully. What did he mean? Presumably that I should have looked outraged and said something like, 'Look here, do you know who you're talking to? I am a highly successful student with a brilliant academic record. How dare you arrest me!' Then they, presumably, would have apologized, perhaps even doffed their caps, and
25 let me on my way.

Two of the paragraphs deal mainly with what happened and two of them with other things. Which ones are which?

Textwork

Understanding
Before you read the text again, make sure you know the meaning of these words and phrases:
    solicitor   costs awarded against the police
    nebulous   the 'right' accent

Unit 3

Now read the passage carefully and answer these questions:
Why did the writer's English teacher come to court?
Did he speak in court? Why (not)?
Why, according to the writer, was he found not guilty?
What particular event does he use as an example to support his argument?
Do you agree with the writer's view?

Vocabulary
1 Explain the meaning of the following phrases as they appear in the text:
conduct my own defence
the magistrate dismissed the case
never stood a chance
had been turned against the police
doffed their caps
2 Now find the words or phrases in the text which mean:
being found not guilty and let go
obviously, and without trying to hide it
sadly/miserably
sorrowfully and accusingly
shocked and insulted, made to become very angry

Showing your attitude

Study
 1 Read the text in Unit 1 (*Squirrel*) again. Decide what the writer mainly wants us to feel. Is it
a sympathetic – this unfortunate event was very unlucky?
b amused – it's an example of the ridiculous things that can sometimes happen in life?
c warned – there are lessons to be learnt from this if we ever find ourselves in a similar situation?
To answer this question consider both the writer's choice of subject-matter and his way of expressing it. What is the emphasis in this story?
For example, if the best answer is *a*, we would expect to find phrases which emphasize how unpleasant the situation *felt*. If the best answer is *b*, we would expect to find phrases which focus on how absurd it *looked*. If *c*, then we would expect to see phrases

which trace an exact chain of cause and effect, and perhaps some general advice.
2 In the first paragraph of *A brush with the law* (Unit 2) you probably noticed two aspects to the writer's attitude: an amused aspect ('makes a good story') and a more serious aspect ('makes it rather disturbing'). These two aspects are emphasized at different points in the story.
a Compare this rewriting of a part of paragraph 5 with the original:
   When I asked what offence I was supposed to have the intention of committing, he told me I was going to steal milk bottles. I was absolutely speechless.
 • Which version shows stronger feeling/is more 'angry'?
 • Which version is more concerned to entertain the reader by being more humorous?
b Now compare this rewriting of a sentence from the text in this unit with its original:
   The stupid police never stood a chance.
Which version is stronger in feeling?
Which version tries to be humorous by pretending to be sympathetic to the police?

Practice
1 Change the attitude shown in the following sentences by choosing the correct alternative (i, ii or iii) according to the instructions.
a One of the policemen who had arrested me was gloomily complaining to my mother that another youngster had been turned against the police.
   Change 'gloomily complaining to' so that the police seem harder and less sympathetic:
   i sadly confessing to
   ii trying to persuade
   iii bitterly commenting to
b 'Get in the back,' they said. 'Put your hands on the back of the front seat and don't move them.'
   Change the second sentence so that the police seem less hard and more ridiculous:
   i They told me to put my hands on the back of the front seat and not to move them.
   ii They insisted I put my hands on the back of the front seat and seemed very worried that I might move them.

iii 'Hands on the back of the front seat. No moving them.'
c Then I made my big mistake. (para. 7 in Unit 2).
This sentence is ironic. Change it to show an attitude which is more genuinely sorry:
  i Then I made a wonderful mistake.
  ii Then I behaved very foolishly.
  iii Then I made a bit of a mistake, with dramatic consequences.
d 'Milk bottles,' he said, and with a perfectly straight face too! (para. 5 in Unit 2).
The second part of this sentence shows the writer's surprise, and also suggests amusement (you can't keep a straight face when something seems very funny to you). Change it to emphasize an attitude of amusement more strongly (after all, it is such a small matter to be serious about).
  i ... as if it were obvious.
  ii ... looking like a TV hero pronouncing the name of the villain.
  iii ... without hesitating for a moment.
e 'Aha,' I could see them thinking, 'unemployed.' (para. 9 in Unit 2).
This sentence makes the police seem rather stupid in jumping to conclusions about the sort of person they had arrested. Change it to make the police seem more reasonable:
  i Naturally, they regarded this as a significant element in the case.
  ii 'I see,' said one of them, his eyes lighting up, 'so you're out of a job, eh?'
  iii For some reason, they seemed to think this was terribly important.

2 You probably realized that the writer of *Squirrel* in Unit 1 had a basically amused attitude to his story. Change the following extracts from the story to show that you regarded the incident as a frightening experience and that your memory of it is not amused but rather unpleasant.
a Restraining myself from making Squirrel-like whines ... (para. 6 in Unit 1).
b Having bumped in an undignified manner down all the steps ... (para. 8 in Unit 1).
c ... as I picked myself up and shook myself ... (para. 8 in Unit 1).

d . . . A road accident? Somebody had attacked me? 'Well, I was rescuing this cat, you see, and . . .' (para. 10 in Unit 1).

Commenting on events

Study
A more direct way of showing your attitude is to comment on events. This is often necessary when you want to make a serious point. The writer in the text of this unit continues to show the same amused attitude as he did in the first part of the story. But when the narrative finishes with his conclusion ('And so I do not have a criminal record'), he becomes more serious and introduces his comment.
Look at the next sentence.
What *exactly* is the writer commenting on?
(Find a particular phrase.)
What *exactly* is his comment about it?
(Find one word.)
In the following sentence the writer goes on to explain his opinion (accent, parents, witnesses, money for a solicitor).
In the sentence after that, the writer supports his argument by hypothesizing about different circumstances. Notice the use of conditional phrases
   IF HAD (BEEN) [DONE] . . . WOULD HAVE (BEEN) [DONE]
which the writer employs to do this.

Practice
In each of the following situations write a few sentences of comment. As in the text, first say what general theme you are commenting on and briefly state your reaction. Then explain your opinion and support your argument by hypothesizing. The first three situations have notes to help you.
1 You went for a job interview as a computer programmer. You were offered the job after an interview of only five minutes. Naturally you were very happy about this. You are very good at your job.
(BUT – rather disturbing – criteria by which I was selected – interviewer was old friend of my father's etc. – might have been very bad at job)

33

Unit 3

2 There was an earthquake in your area. It was a strong earthquake but there were very few casualties because the buildings are well built.
(BUT – scandalous – no official emergency procedures – nobody with responsibility could be found to give advice on TV or radio – most people spent night on ground floor of flats or just outside – wrong: most dangerous place – if another earthquake soon afterwards, thousands of deaths)
3 John Smith passed an exam by only one mark when he was eleven years old. Because he passed, he went to a very good secondary school. There the teaching was very good and he got a lot of personal attention. As a result, John got a place at a very good university and now he is a very successful architect.
(only one mark – teaching at some secondary schools very poor)
4 You are the writer of *Squirrel* in Unit 1. You stayed in hospital for two days but luckily you did not get any delayed concussion. While you were there, the nurses came to see you only twice and a doctor only once.
5 You needed to send some money to your mother in another country; she urgently needed an operation. To do this you had to go to the national bank to arrange the transfer. All the banks in the city were on strike, but you managed to make the transfer quickly because a top official in the national bank is your personal friend.

Extended writing

1 Use the notes below to write a short essay. Before you start writing, decide what attitude you are going to take. When you write the story show your attitude by describing the events in a way which makes this clear. Finish your essay by commenting on the events, using the information in brackets at the end of the notes, and/or any other information you want to invent.
   went to see friend, doctor in large hospital
   had piece of paper with her signature on it (to show I was a friend)
   showed paper to porter at hospital
   porter looked and thought
   couldn't help
   told me to go to reception
   reception unable to help
   told me to go to admissions desk

admissions desk signed piece of paper
told me to go to third floor
nurse took paper
signed it
told me to get into bed
ignored my protests
got help from other nurses
found bed for me
forced me into bed
. . .
friend came two hours later
explained to nurses, released, all OK

(bed they put me in was last empty bed in hospital – it was a holiday weekend, lots of traffic accidents)

2 Write one of the following essays.
a Your own account of a brush with the law.
b Describe an encounter with bureaucracy.
c An extremely lucky coincidence and its consequences.

Unit 4
Writing letters of protest
Sir!

Reading practice

🔑 Below is a letter of protest to a newspaper (which is called *The News*). It is common for editors to give titles to the letters they publish. Read the letter as fast as you can and decide which of the following would be the best title for it.
    Medical Certificates   The Office Cat
    Authorities too Cautious Bureaucats

                                          Camdale
                                         1 July 19. .

1 Sir,
    It is good news that the government is trying to eliminate unnecessary red tape (*News*, 14 April), but a recent experience of mine would suggest that not much has been done yet.

2 I wanted to send a cat out of the country. On the phone the veterinary office at the airport told me I would need to show them a certificate of recent medical examination and a certificate of rabies vaccination. But when I went to the airport with these documents the vet refused to see me. He had neglected to tell me that the public was not admitted after 11.30.

3 I managed to arrive earlier the next day, but the vet peremptorily refused to give me export clearance. Apparently, the record of rabies vaccination had to be on the certificate of examination and not, as I had it, on a separate document. He dismissed me and told me that next time I'd better bring the animal as well.

4 Luckily, I had to return only five minutes later because I had left my wallet in his office. I say 'luckily' because this time I was informed that my certificate was unacceptable anyway because it was not in English.

5 A few days later (my third attempt), armed with new documentation and the cat, approval was still not forthcoming. I was told that I should have filled in an application form. This was the first I had heard of any application, but apparently it was my fault for not making one before.

6 After much protesting on my part, the vet graciously made an exception and granted me clearance. Finally, my cat had permission to travel.

7 I had never imagined that the export of a cat was of such vital importance to the nation as to warrant such 'caution' on the part of the authorities. I can understand a certain amount of red tape being necessary. The country does not want to get a reputation as an exporter of disease. However, the trail of misinformation and obstructiveness which I had to follow cannot be described as 'necessary'. In fact it could have had a traumatic effect on my whole life.

8 This is not an exaggeration. The number of days I had to have off work, at short notice, nearly led to my losing the job!
                              Yours faithfully,
                              Robert Wood

Unit 4

Textwork

Understanding
Before you read the letter again, make sure you understand these words
    red tape   rabies   vaccination   vet
When you have read it, answer these questions:
Why did the writer need to see the airport vet?
Why did he fail the first time he went?
Why did he fail the second time?
In what sense was he 'lucky' to have forgotten his wallet?
Why did he nearly fail the third time?
Why didn't he have to go a fourth time?
What, exactly, is the writer protesting about?

Vocabulary
Find the words or phrases in the text which mean:
    get rid of/stop
    forgotten, out of laziness
    very quickly and suddenly
    permission to proceed
    justify
    making things difficult for people to achieve

Being ironic

Study
1 Answer these questions (look at paras. 5 and 6):
Was it really the writer's fault that he had not made an application in writing?
Do you think the vet was really being gracious when he granted clearance?
The writer uses words such as
    apparently   graciously   luckily
as a way of ironically emphasizing his difficulties. Here are four more words which are sometimes used in the same way:
    obviously   reassuringly
    pleasantly   helpfully
2 Now look at paragraph 7. Here, the writer uses another way of being ironic. Answer this question:

Do you think the export of a cat is really 'of such vital importance to the nation'?
By using the phrase
I had never imagined. . .
the writer pretends to be surprised at a new discovery he has just made. The reader understands that he is only pretending and that what he has 'discovered' is not, in fact, true. Here are some more phrases which can be used in this way:
I would never have thought . . .
I had no idea . . .
I had not realized
Can you think of any others?

Practice

1 In each of the following sentences, a word is missing. Choose from the list of ironic adverbs in the *Study* section on page 37 to fill in the gap. (Remember, you may need to work by a process of elimination and answer the questions in a different order.)
a 'So you don't believe in God?' said the dentist _____ as he approached me with the drill.
b After registering great disapproval, my boss _____ let me have the day off to go to my mother's funeral.
c 'Don't worry,' he said _____ as I was about to jump out of the plane, 'most parachutes usually open.'
d The police saw that I had long untidy hair. _____ I was going to steal milk bottles.
e The love of my life had just got married to somebody else. Larry _____ suggested I should take up stamp collecting.
f The driver's lawyer started to criticize me: _____ I should have been looking when the car came up on to the pavement.

2 In the following situations use the phrases in the *Study* section above to make an ironic comment.
Example: The police have been trying to find a criminal with green eyes. You have green eyes. The police arrested you. It was two days before they realized you were not the person they were looking for.
Comment: I had no idea that having green eyes was such a danger.
a You went to see a friend who was a doctor in a hospital. You were mistaken for a patient and made to get into bed.
b While you were in your car you were stopped by the police. When they saw an old-fashioned starting handle in the back of the car they arrested you for carrying an offensive weapon.

c In an interview for a high-powered job as 'Personal Assistant', the manager offered your sister the job as soon as he found out that her husband was a long-distance lorry driver.
d The customs officer opened your case and began to look through it. 'What team do you support?' he asked conversationally. 'Manchester United,' you replied. Immediately he closed the case and let you go through. If he had continued looking he would have found all the bottles of perfume you were carrying.
e The *Daily News* has always stressed the need for more motorways in the country. But it strongly objects to a new proposal for a motorway that would mean the demolition of several historic buildings. You happen to know that the editor's house is one of these buildings.

Anticipating objections to your argument

Study
When you are expressing a point of view you can often be more effective if you imagine how other people might disagree with you. The writer of the letter to *The News* is arguing against bureaucracy. He realizes that people could answer him by saying something like, 'Yes, but bureaucracy is always necessary.'
a What are the two sentences in the letter where he shows he is aware of this, and why?
Then he makes a claim that the events nearly had a disastrous effect on his life. He realizes that some people might find this a bit ridiculous.
b What is the sentence which shows he is aware of this?
Here are some ways to anticipate a disagreement:

I can understand . . .
It is true that . . .   (when the opposite opinion which
Certainly . . .   follows is fairly natural and obvious)

One could argue that . . . (when the opposite opinion is more sophisticated)

This is not an exaggeration.   (in answer to the charge
This is not just fanciful thinking.   that your opinion is in some way ridiculous)

Having anticipated objections, you can then proceed to deal with them. How does the writer deal with the two objections mentioned above?

39

Unit 4

Practice
Now practise the same thing by making the notes below into connected sentences.
1 nurses stupid to refuse to believe I was *not* a patient – patients can't always be believed – could have seen I was perfectly healthy – (Besides) might have cost someone their life – made me get into last empty bed in whole hospital.
2 country on brink of disaster – studies show too much unemployment can rip the fabric of society – direct result of government's economic policy – international factors beyond government's control – these factors largely the same under previous government.
3 not enough buses in the city – taxis do the job – expensive and unreliable.
4 owing to pollution, city becoming major disaster area – London 1952, 4,000 deaths as result of pollution – clean-up would be too expensive – either that or eventually abandon whole city.
5 might have died in that hospital and nobody noticed – 'under observation' but was not observed once in forty-eight hours – obviously OK when admitted – why was I kept there at all?
6 nearly found guilty just because father a famous criminal – small offence, would not have gone to prison – would have had criminal record and consequent disadvantages – police lawyer placed great emphasis on my father's reputation.

Extended writing

1 You are the person who was arrested for loitering with intent to commit an arrestable offence. You have decided to write a letter to *The News* protesting at what you see as inequalities in the law. Begin your letter like this:
Sir,
   The law is supposed to apply equally to everybody. Last year, however, . . .
Then use your summaries of the story to give the relevant details of what happened. After that, make your claim about inequality and support it by anticipating and answering objections. Make any other comments which you feel are relevant (you may find it possible to be ironic!).
2 Write *one* of the following letters:
a A letter complaining about your local bus service. You have

Unit 4

already written to the bus company but they have not been at all helpful.
b Look back at the hospital situation at the end of the last unit. Then look at the references to the same situation in the exercises in this unit. Write a letter of protest.

Unit 5
Writing about an incident IV
Earthquake

Reading practice
Below are three paragraphs from an essay which describes an earthquake. After writing them, the writer decided to add some phrases to describe his feelings and reactions to the events. These are the phrases:
  It felt as if some awful giant was giving the building a good shake.
  I didn't pay much attention to it.
  I had a terrible feeling of helplessness.
  I wasn't particularly concerned.
  At any rate, I had been disabused of the idea that it was just another lorry.
  In fact, I was mildly annoyed.
  For a moment we sat motionless, transfixed with horror, shock or both.
Now here are the paragraphs. Each time you see a number, put in one of the phrases above.

   I had just opened another drink and was pouring it out when I heard a faint rumbling noise. At the time . . . (1) . . . Even when the noise got louder and the windows began to rattle . . . (2) . . . (3) . . . I assumed it was an unusually heavy lorry coming up the road and I was just about to come out with a few choice expletives directed at vehicles like this when the cups in the kitchen and the jars on the shelf began to rattle as well.
   I don't remember which one of us was the first to realize it was an earthquake . . . (4) . . . By this time everything inside the flat was shaking, rattling or wobbling, including the walls, ceiling and floor . . . (5) . . .
   . . . (6) . . . Then we all sprang to our feet, with what purpose I can't really say. Not that it did much good anyway, as we were all promptly thrown back into our seats . . . (7) . . .

Textwork

Understanding
First check that you know these words:
  rumble   rattle   wobble   aftershock
Now read the whole of the story and answer the questions which follow it.

1   It was eleven o'clock on Tuesday evening. The three of us were sitting round in the living room after supper. I had just opened another bottle and was pouring it out when I heard a faint rumbling noise. At the time, I didn't pay much attention to it. Even when the noise got louder and the windows

began to rattle I wasn't particularly concerned. In fact, I was mildly annoyed. I assumed it was an unusually heavy lorry coming up the road and I was just about to come out with a few choice expletives directed at vehicles like this when the cups in the kitchen and the jars on the shelf began to rattle as well.

2   I don't remember which one of us was the first to realize it was an earthquake. At any rate, I had been disabused of the idea that it was just another lorry. By this time everything inside the flat was shaking, rattling or wobbling, including the walls, ceiling and floor. It felt as if some awful giant was venting his anger by holding the building and giving it a good shake.

3   For a moment, we sat motionless, transfixed with horror, shock or both. Then we all sprang to our feet, with what purpose I can't really say. Not that it did much good anyway, as we were all promptly thrown back into our seats. I had a terrible feeling of helplessness.

4   At a second attempt, we managed to stay on our feet and started making for the open door out on to the balcony. When we got there we saw that there had been a power cut and the whole city had been plunged into darkness. By this time the shaking had stopped and everything seemed curiously still and quiet. For a moment it seemed as if a hand had passed over the city and extinguished it like a candle. Although it had seemed like hours, the quake had only lasted ten seconds or so.

5   Gradually, the sounds of life began again – horns tooting, windows opening, voices. I don't remember any screaming or shouting. Everything was strangely muted, disturbed rather than desperate.

6   After a while, we went back into the house. There was no obvious damage. A few books had fallen out of the shelves and the only thing broken was an egg cup. As we listened for news on the radio over the next few hours, we realized we had been very lucky. People nearby had had televisions and stereos smashed, and several villages outside the city had been virtually flattened. Most people spent that night outside. Some people had to spend weeks outside because their homes had been damaged.

7   We didn't. We lived at the top of a building, which is the safest place to be in an earthquake, so we stayed put. At three o'clock we even went to bed, which is where we were when the first big aftershock came about two hours later.

    It was quite a night.

What was the first sign of the earthquake?
What was the second? And the third? And the fourth?
What was the writer's first reaction? Why?
When did the writer realize it was not just a lorry?
What did the writer and his friends do then?
Apart from the description of the shaking etc., what indication is there that the earthquake was quite strong?

Unit 5

How much damage did the earthquake cause?
Why didn't the writer go down to the street?

Vocabulary
1 Explain the meaning of these phrases as they appear in the text:
   a few choice expletives
   I had been disabused of the idea
   venting his anger
   a power cut
   virtually flattened
2 Now find the words or phrases in the text which mean:
   quiet/at a very low volume
   unable to move, as if stuck
   stood up very quickly
   going towards, with purpose
   made completely dark
   didn't go away from where we were

Describing feelings and impressions

Study
Look at the phrases you used during the *Reading practice*. In them, the writer describes his feelings and impressions (he does not describe what happened). To do this is particularly important when you want the reader to feel what it was like to be in the same situation.
Notice the use of *metaphor* in the phrase
   transfixed with horror.
Literally, 'transfixed' means to be pinned, stuck or nailed across something (e.g. a wall). Obviously the writer was not really in this situation. The word is being used in a non-literal, 'poetic' sense. This is metaphor.
Can you find another metaphor in the third paragraph?
Notice also the use of *simile* in the phrase
   It *felt as if* some awful giant . . .
The writer has compared what was happening with something else. This is simile. A common way to begin a simile is with
   a verb of the senses (e.g. looked, seemed)
followed by
   as if, as though *or* like (first person only).

Unit 5

Can you find another simile in the fourth paragraph? Both metaphor and simile are useful ways to make your description more vivid and dramatic.

Practice
1 Match the following situations (a-f) with the most suitable description of feelings and impressions (i-vi). (Read all of the situations first.)
a You had been on a long-distance coach for several days. During this time you had no opportunity for a wash or a change of clothes.
b You were reading a list of the names of people who had won a scholarship to university. The list was in alphabetical order and you had just got to the letter which your name begins with (you wanted to go to university very much).
c You had been waiting in the dentist's waiting room. Then the dentist asked you to come in (you are absolutely terrified of dentists).
d You went to work feeling extremely ill and having had only two hours' sleep for the last two nights.
e You used to be a fanatical supporter of a certain football team. This team had just lost a very important match to a team everyone expected it to beat.
f You opened the door and found *both* your girl/boyfriends standing there (neither of them knew of the other's existence).
 i I felt a sinking feeling in my stomach.
 ii My heart missed a beat.
 iii I must have looked as though I'd been dragged through a hedge backwards.
 iv It seemed to me as if the world had come to an end.
 v I felt like death warmed up.
 vi I felt like a cornered rat.
2 Now try to make suitable one-sentence descriptions of your feelings and impressions for the following situations. You may use metaphor, simile and/or a simple statement.
a You went to visit a very untidy friend. There had been a party at his/her house the night before. Also, your friend was getting ready to move house and had started packing. Describe the living room.
b You visited a village that had just suffered a very bad earthquake.
c You came back home after two weeks' holiday. It was a very,

45

very hot day and all the windows in the house had been closed while you were away.
d You were waiting on the platform for a train. When the train came it was absolutely packed with thousands of people.
e You had just asked for the bill at a restaurant when you realized you had left all your money at home.

Connecting past events

Study
1   The texts in the previous units dealt with events that took place over several hours. The text in this unit describes a very dramatic event. The first five paragraphs cover no more than a minute of real time.
To allow us to feel the dramatic nature of the event the writer has to slow things down, rather like a film camera in slow motion.
Note the following ways the writer 'stretches' time:
a In the first two paragraphs none of the verb phrases describe a completed event. There are many *continuous* tenses (*shake, rattle, wobble, vent, hold, give* in the second paragraph). There are also verbs which describe a progression (*get, begin* in the first paragraph).
b In the second paragraph you can see the phrase 'by this time', which emphasizes that time has passed and things have been happening. Find it again later in the text.
c *Between* the descriptions of events in the text there is a lot of description of personal feeling and reaction.
2   Another way in which the writer can help us to feel the drama of events is to use phrases which pinpoint an exact moment.
a Study the use of 'just' in phrases expressing interrupted action in the first paragraph.
b Notice the use of 'for a moment'.

Practice

1   In each of the following questions, one action is interrupted by another. Make good sentences from them, using 'just' where appropriate and being careful about the tense.
a get in the bath – telephone ring.
b make a phone call – realize the phone was not connected.
c walk along the street – hear somebody call me.
d cross the road – hear a voice calling my name from behind me on the other side.

e cross the road – notice a car coming along very fast.
f drop off to sleep – be woken by a terrible noise.
g doze comfortably in front of the TV – felt everything start to shake.
(NOTICE THAT THE TENSE OFTEN DEPENDS ON THE MEANING OF THE VERB AND/OR THE WHOLE SENTENCE.)
2 Make the following sets of circumstances into coherent paragraphs by using a suitable tense and/or using verbs of progression where appropriate in order to 'stretch' the period of time. Make other additions and/or changes where necessary.
a (the last hundred metres or so of the Olympic 10,000 metres) come round last bend – Packard well in front – he tire – still looked a certain winner – Voicek gain ground – crowd roar – run neck and neck for last twenty metres – crowd rise to its feet – shout as if it had one voice – in last second Voicek inch ahead.
b As I passed the shelf I felt my arm brush against something – turn round – precious vase wobble – for a moment, feeling of helplessness – run to catch it – topple over – catch it before it hit floor.
c My car had stalled. There I was stuck in the middle of the road – other car come towards me very fast – not really worried – obvious it going to hit me – life flash before my eyes – hit me – my car spin round – windscreen come out – seem like a dream – spin for years – wake up from dream, car not spinning – other car stop too – shake myself – get out of car.

Extended writing

1 Use the following notes as the basis for a short description of a storm. Most of the notes concentrate on the action (the things that happened). You should try to add personal feelings, impressions and reactions wherever you think suitable, using your own ideas and/or the suggestions for these at the end of the notes.
middle of the night
have disturbing dream for quite some time
wake up (think I heard very loud noise)
wonder what it was – great flash outside window
continual rumble in distance
went outside
very strong wind

awnings flap, things bang around
rumble much louder, lightning every few seconds
could hear sea even though ten miles away
full force of storm hit us
awnings torn out of their supports, glass shattered
rain, went inside
have to fight to shut door against wind
rain stronger
hailstones drum on window
sit and watch
patio flooded in ten minutes

alternately frightening and exciting
seemed like broad daylight
city like a ship in a rough sea
building felt as fragile as a vase

2 Write an essay about *one* of the following.
a An account of extreme weather conditions in which you were personally involved.
b An account of a natural disaster in which you were personally involved.
c An account of a demonstration or a mass rally.

Unit 6
News reporting
Disaster

Reading practice
The text below is a newspaper report. Imagine that you are the editor of the newspaper.
1 Read the report and find a headline for it of between fourteen and twenty characters (each letter, punctuation mark, and space between words counts as one 'character').

Since the beginning of this month Britain has been experiencing one of its worst winters in recorded history, and all the signs are that it will continue.
The first snowfall of the winter usually causes one or two days of temporary chaos, but this time the British are finding it particularly hard to adapt to such inclement weather conditions. Hospitals have reported thousands of cases of broken arms and legs from people who were trying simply to walk on the ice-covered streets. These have become so dangerous that yesterday police in London modified their constant warning of 'Don't go out unless you have to' to a stark 'Don't go out'.
Public transport facilities have been severely affected. Even where roads are passable, buses and long-distance coaches often have to be cancelled owing to lack of staff. Police report that another heavy snowfall yesterday evening in the west of the country led to hundreds of cars being abandoned along the main road to Plymouth in Devonshire.
London's Heathrow Airport is, however, operating normally. Special equipment is able to keep the runways ice-free. Electricity and gas supplies are also holding up and there is no immediate danger of a power shortage.
Two days ago the thermometer in Glasgow, Scotland, read minus 26 degrees Celsius (−26°C), the lowest temperature ever recorded in the British Isles since records first began to be kept a hundred years ago.
In Cambridge, fifty miles north of London, the workers at a sausage factory have taken to spending their break times in the large deep-freeze compartment. This is kept at a constant temperature of −4°C, and the workers claim it is warmer than anywhere else!

2 Newspaper articles have to fit into an allotted space. The original article was slightly too long for the space and before it went to press the editor took out the following phrases. Decide where in the article they come from.
a Rail connections in the north-west of the country have been virtually non-existent for a week.
b Apart from delays in the baggage-reclaim section, where the conveyor belts have frozen several times.
c A strong anti-cyclone is entrenched over the British Isles, bringing Siberian and Arctic conditions to most parts of the country.

49

Unit 6

d The cold, clear weather has meant that it has been mercifully free of fog, so often a cause of delays for passengers in winter.

Textwork

Understanding
Read the passage carefully and answer the following questions.
Does the text suggest that the British are normally prepared for bad winter weather?
What is implied about the weather conditions from the two police warnings?
Does the text suggest that some roads are impassable?
What two possible reasons could there be for a bus or a coach being cancelled?
Why do you think that power supplies and the airport are mentioned together in the same paragraph?
How could it possibly be 'warmer' inside a deep-freeze compartment?

Vocabulary
1 Explain the meaning of these words and phrases as they appear in the text:
all the signs are that it will continue
modified (their constant warning)
owing to (lack of staff)
(gas supplies are also) holding up
have taken to spending
2 Now find the words in the text which mean:
unkind, uncomfortable
simple, direct, bald
can be used (for a route)
left behind on purpose
the place where aeroplanes land and take off

Moving from general to particular

Study
1 The article deals with a number of aspects of how the bad weather has affected the country.
Look at the second paragraph. What is the main theme here? Find a particular phrase.

The writer then goes on to give an example of this generalization. This is the second sentence.
The third sentence is even more particular; it mentions something which happened at a particular time as a direct result of the facts we have been told in the second sentence.
In this paragraph we thus have three levels of generality:
  First   – people finding it difficult to adapt
  Second   – thousands of broken arms and legs
  Third   – police warning yesterday
This movement to more particular statements is a common progression in any piece of writing where the main function is to provide information.
Look at the third paragraph and identify three similar levels of generality.
Sometimes, however, a paragraph might take a backward step. Look at the fourth paragraph. Here, the scheme is:
  First level   – airport OK
  Second level – special equipment for runways
  First level   – electricity and gas OK
This grouping of two 'first-level' themes in the same paragraph is because they have something very relevant in common; they are working normally, unlike everything else which is mentioned in the article.
2 Study the use of verb tenses in the second and third paragraphs. Relate them to the levels of generality which you have studied. Notice that:
a there are only two examples of the simple past tense [DID]. In each case it appears at the level of greatest particularity;
b levels of greater generality may have a variety of tenses but perfect tenses [HAVE/HAD (BEEN) DONE] and continuous tenses [BE DOING] are common.
This progression from a perfect or a continuous tense to the simple past tense is very common in a story or report in just the same way as it is very common to progress from the general to the particular.

Practice
The following selections of facts are taken from newspaper articles. Put each of them into a suitable order and then write a good news paragraph. Be careful with the tenses!
1 capital city without telephones for five hours yesterday
   no public transport for several days now

communications badly affected by civil war
2 crops failed last year, signs are fail again
international relief organizations attempt to get supplies to afflicted areas
Western Renialand – one of worst droughts this century
no rain for more than a year
danger of mass starvation
3 some areas under a foot of water or more
power supplies severely affected
whole city without power yesterday
city in chaos
power restored to most areas by now
one woman drowned in a major city street, trapped in car
4 rescue work started, little hope of survivors
slag engulfed schoolhouse in seconds
44 schoolchildren thought dead
slag heap above village of Aberfan, South Wales, collapsed
thought caused by heavy rains
5 thousands spend night outdoors for fear of further shocks
city reeling from series of earth tremors
several buildings badly damaged
tremor 5 a.m. causes large crack in outer wall of Hilton Hotel

Note: mass starvation = large numbers of people dying of hunger
afflicted = suffering, badly affected
slag heap = mountain made of the waste material from coal mining
tremor = comparatively small earthquake
reeling = shocked, thrown off balance

Summarizing

Study
How you make a text shorter depends on two things:
a exactly how short your version has to be
b the purpose of your summary.
Imagine you have been told to produce a short paragraph of only about forty words about the winter weather in Britain. If you think this is the first your readers have heard about the conditions in Britain you will want to provide 'news', and all you can do in forty words is record the main facts. You would probably produce something like this:

Unusually severe winter weather in Britain has caused thousands of cases of broken limbs from people slipping on the ice, cancellation of at least half of scheduled bus and coach journeys and hundreds of cars to be abandoned. Airports and power supplies have not been affected.

Notice that what is included is mostly from the middle level of generality of the original article. It does not include the most general statements (people finding it hard to adapt, transport being severely affected), which do not have much meaning unless they are followed by exemplification. Also, the summary does not include the most particular statements (police warning yesterday, police report of snowfall yesterday evening, special equipment for airport runways), which, on their own, do not communicate the main effects of the weather.

Notice also that the summary includes nothing from the last two paragraphs of the original article. That is because they are largely anecdotal. Paragraph 5 says nothing about the effects of the weather, and paragraph 6 cannot really be understood unless the readers already know many of the facts in the original article.

But if the readers know about the terrible weather in Britain, your editor might ask for forty words of 'human interest'. In that case you might write:

People in Britain are finding bizarre ways of coping with the freezing weather. Workers at a factory in Cambridge spend their break times in the deep-freeze compartment. They claim it is warmer than anywhere else!

Practice
1 Your editor wants a 'news' article about the winter weather in Britain of between 90 and 110 words. Make sure that you include the most important facts and that your article makes sense as a whole.
2 The next day your editor wants another article of the same length about the conditions in Britain in winter. Now your readers know the main facts, so this time a 'human interest' story is wanted which emphasizes what it is like to be in Britain at this time.

Extended writing

1 You have to write an article of between 275 and 300 words on an earthquake which has recently occurred in Greece. It is a major

Unit 6

article and, like the article at the beginning of this unit, should include both important facts and also more anecdotal information of human interest. To write the article use the text in Unit 5 and some or all of the following information:
  earthquake central Greece, 11 p.m. last night
  6.8 on Richter scale, epicentre near Corinth
  two villages destroyed
  large hotel near Corinth collapsed
    (300 tourists had been due to arrive next week)
  hundreds of buildings in Athens damaged
    (Athens sixty kilometres away)
  people ran out of houses and flats in panic
  half population spent night in squares or cars
  roads jammed, many people fleeing city
  hundreds of aftershocks recorded since first quake
  experts say worst is over
  inspection of buildings to begin tomorrow
  expected hundreds made effectively homeless
  government providing tents
  twenty people known to have died (mostly from panic, jumping out of third-storey windows, heart attacks etc.)
  city very quiet today
  more than half of offices, shops, factories not working
2 Write one of the following articles:
a About 250 words on another earthquake.
b About 250 words on a flood.
c About 200 words on the result of an election which has just taken place in a foreign country (you will find useful vocabulary in the next unit).

Follow the instructions about the number of words closely. You are writing a newspaper article and there is only a certain amount of space available.

Unit 7
Academic essay/report – process
Elections

Reading practice
The essay below is a description of how the electoral system in Britain works. After writing the essay the writer decided to take out a number of phrases; he thought they were either not directly relevant to the description or not necessary for its understanding. These are the phrases:
a where people vote.
b who tend to have a much greater proportion of seats in Parliament than the proportion of votes they received.
c This is a list of the names of all the people entitled to vote in the constituency.
d who is usually a local government official.
e The aim of this is to discourage frivolous candidatures; that is, people standing as candidates for a joke or for cheap publicity.
Now read the essay and decide at exactly what point each of these phrases appeared before they were taken out.

The type of electoral system in operation in Britain at a national level is known as the relative majority system. Many complaints have been made about its unfairness, which discriminates in favour of major parties. It has the advantage, however, of being very simple and straightforward.

The country is divided into 650 electoral areas which are called constituencies. Each constituency returns one Member of Parliament to Westminster. The person responsible for the conduct of the election in each constituency is known as the Returning Officer.

When a date for the election has been fixed, nominations for candidates in each constituency are invited. To be a candidate, it is necessary to produce ten signatures of electors in the constituency and to deposit £150 with the Returning Officer. The candidate forfeits this deposit if he or she fails to poll at least 12 per cent of the total vote.

Nominations close ten working days before the date of the election. The ballot papers can then be printed. These are the papers on which the voters mark their choice. They contain only the name of each candidate, the candidate's home address and a short 'political description' of the candidate. In practice, this means the name of the political party which he or she represents.

The day before the election, the ballot papers are distributed to the polling stations in the constituency. Each elector is registered to vote at a particular polling station.

Election Day is always a Thursday. The polls open at 7 a.m. and close at 10 p.m. At the polling station an elector is first ticked off on the electoral register and then given a ballot paper. The elector then takes the paper to a polling booth, where he or she can make a choice in secret. Voting is done simply by putting an 'X' next to the name of the preferred candidate. Having voted, the elector folds the ballot paper and drops it into a ballot box.

Unit 7

(Note: This is not the end of the process. *You* will continue the description in the next unit.)

Textwork

Understanding
Make sure you understand what is meant by 'electoral system' and then read the text again carefully and answer these questions:
Does everybody in Britain think that their electoral system is a good one?
Is it necessary to belong to a political party in order to be a candidate?
Do candidates have to pay a fee to enter the election?
Is it necessary to be on the electoral register before you can vote?
How many ballot papers is each elector given?
How many choices does each elector make?

Vocabulary
Explain as exactly as possible the meaning of these words and phrases as they appear in the text.
 constituency
 (each constituency) returns
 Returning Officer
 nominations for candidates
 ballot papers

 political description
 polling station
 electoral register
 polling booth
 ballot box

Using and explaining specialist terms

Study
When writing academically or technically, you may have to use vocabulary which is usually only used with the subject matter of your essay or report (e.g. 'ballot paper'). You may also use words or phrases which, although they exist in the everyday language, have a particular meaning in this specialized context (e.g. 'returns'). In these cases it is obviously important to make sure that your reader understands exactly what these terms refer to (or that your professor can see that *you* understand!).
Look at your answers to the *Vocabulary* exercise in the *Textwork*. Probably you did not find it very difficult, because the writer tried to make himself clear. Three ways of doing this can be seen in the text. They are:

1 PRE-EXPLANATION: ... BE called / known as X.

2 POST-EXPLANATION: X BE ... / This/These mean(s) ...

3 CONTEXT: the meaning of the term can be inferred, especially if it is an object and some information is given on its use.

Study again the terms in the *Vocabulary* section as they appear in the text. Which of these methods was used to help the reader in each case?

There is also another method of explanation. This is

4 EQUIVALENCE: providing a paraphrase immediately after the first appearance of the term. An example can be seen in *e* of the *Reading practice* at the beginning of this unit.

Practice

1 Provide one-sentence explanations for each of the terms below, following the instructions in each case.

a ballot paper   – use pre-explanation
b ballot paper   – use explanation by context
c polling station   – use pre-explanation
d polling station   – use post-explanation
e political description   – use pre-explanation
f political description   – use explanation by equivalence
g constituency   – use explanation by context
h constituency   – use explanation by equivalence
i electoral register   – use post-explanation
j Returning Officer   – use post-explanation

2 Write a short description of the game of football for someone who knows nothing about it. Use the framework below and the explanations immediately below that. You will have to decide which method of explaining is the most useful in each case, and you may sometimes expect the reader to understand what you mean from the context.

    two teams, eleven players each
    rectangular field about 100 metres long
    at each end, a goal
    aim of game to score goals
    not allowed to touch ball with hands or arms
    if foul committed, other team awarded free kick
    if foul inside penalty area, penalty awarded
    if one team puts ball outside boundaries of pitch, other team takes goal kick or throw in

Unit 7

game controlled by referee
game usually 90 minutes (= 2 × 45) + 15 minutes' half-time
pitch rectangular field on which game is played
goal archway about 7.5 metres wide by 2.5 metres high
score a goal make the ball go into the goal
commit a foul break the rules of the game
free kick one team is given possession of the ball and the other team is not allowed to interfere until the first team has kicked it
take a penalty a member of the attacking team attempts to score a goal by kicking from only about ten metres away. Only the defending goalkeeper may try to stop this
penalty area area inside which a penalty may be awarded
goalkeeper member of the team whose job is to prevent the other team scoring. Unlike all the others, he is allowed to handle the ball
take a throw in put the ball back into play by throwing into the playing area after it has gone outside the sides of the pitch
take a goal kick put the ball back into play by kicking it after it has gone outside the ends of the pitch
referee person who decides when and if a foul has been committed, which team has the right to the ball, whether a goal has been scored etc.
half-time interval between the first and second periods of the game

Impersonal verbal constructions

Study
In academic descriptions of processes and systems, people, as agents of actions, are not often important. The reader is interested in 'things'.
In the text here, two features are common in the verb phrases.
1 Passive forms, e.g. IS DONE/ARE DONE/CAN BE DONE.
How many passive verb phrases are there in the text?
Find the phrases in the text which correspond to the following phrases:
Printers can print the ballot papers.
The Returning Officer distributes the ballot papers.
Each elector can vote at the polling station where his or her name is written down on a list.
2 'Active fallacies'. Here, through the choice of verb, the subject,

which is impersonal, appears to be the active agent even when it is not.
e.g. Each constituency returns one Member of Parliament to Westminster.
A constituency does not really 'do' anything; what we really mean is the people in a constituency.
There are two other verb phrases later on in the text which have the same feature. Can you find them?

Practice
Turn the following sequence of facts into a coherent piece of writing. Make use of passive forms, 'active fallacies' (where appropriate) and use sequencing phrases such as 'Next', 'Then', 'After that' etc. (or, if you want to be more sophisticated, turn to the next unit to find out more about sequencing!).

People drink a lot of tea in Britain.
People do not grow tea in Britain.
   (People cannot grow tea in Britain – it is too cold.)
People grow tea in hot countries.
India is a hot country.
People grow tea on hillsides.
People pick only the top leaves of the plant.
People leave the leaves in the sun.
The sun dries the leaves.
People put the leaves into boxes.
People ship the boxes to London.
Tea merchants in London buy the tea.
People put the tea into packets or tins.
People distribute the tea to shops throughout Britain.

Extended writing

1 On the next page there is a flow diagram which attempts to summarize criminal procedure in Britain. The words in the diagram describe what happens to a person who the police think has committed a crime (the words in brackets describe where the event takes place). The arrows show the order in which the events happen. Notice that in some cases there is more than one possibility. Arrows going nowhere mean that the person concerned is now free. Below the diagram is a glossary of specialist terms.

Unit 7

Use
a the information in the diagram
b the glossary (to explain specialist terms when the context does not make the meaning clear)
c the language you have practised in this unit (where appropriate) and sequencing phrases
to write a short introduction to criminal procedure in Britain.

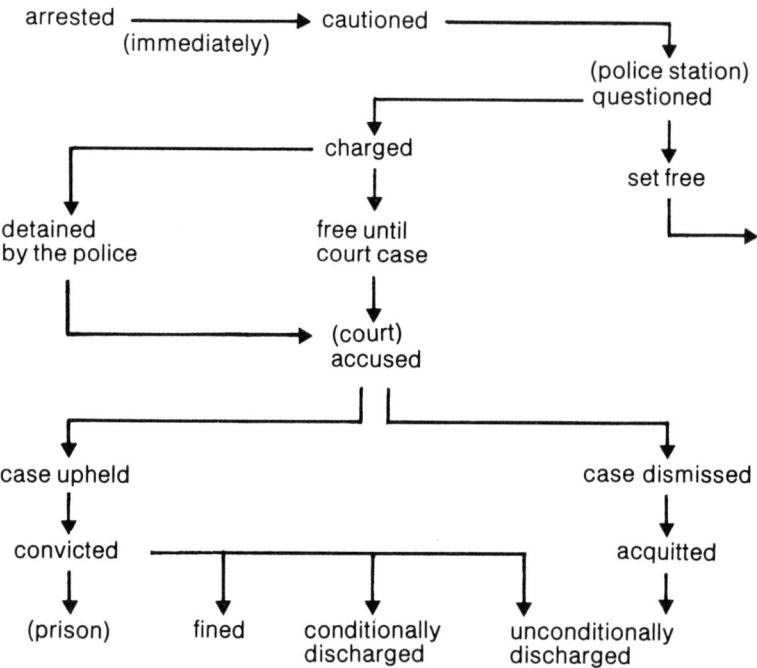

arrest the person is not free, must stay with the police until told otherwise.
caution official warning by police of person's rights and possible consequences of anything said. Standard formula. Arrest not legal without it.
charge official claim that person has committed a particular crime.
acquitted the person is innocent or it has *not* been proved that he/she committed a crime.
convicted it *has* been proved that the accused committed a crime.

conditionally discharged the person is freed without punishment, but if he/she commits another crime within a stated time, this first crime will be taken into account.
fine sum of money, to be paid as a punishment.

2 Write an account of *one* of the following:
a The electoral system *or* criminal procedure in your country.
b A traditional yearly celebration in your country.
c A scientific process with which you are familiar.

Unit 8
Academic essay/report – narrative
The end of the Saxon kings

Reading practice
Below you will find three extracts from paragraphs 3, 4 and 6 of an essay recounting some of the events of 1066, the most famous date in English history. Read them and decide which paragraph is which.

a   But this was not his only danger. His disaffected brother Tosti had formed an alliance with Harold Hardraada, king of Norway, who also had designs on the English throne. He also had prepared an invasion fleet and on 19 September this fleet, having ravaged much of the north-eastern coastline, disembarked near York. On the next day, the invaders defeated the northern earls at Fulford Gate. At the same time, Harold left London with an army to repulse them. Four days later, while Harold was still marching north, Hardraada was accepted as king of northern England at York. But his 'reign' proved to be short-lived. The following day the two armies met and engaged in a great battle at Stamford Bridge . . .

b   For the next week, while Harold's tired army was marching south, without its bowmen and cavalry, the Norman invaders were consolidating their position on the south coast, ravaging the countryside around Hastings and . . .

c   As soon as he heard this news, William sent envoys to Harold to remind him of his oath. Harold bluntly denied William's claims, and the stage was set. By the end of the month, William had begun preparations to take the throne by force of arms . . .

Sequencing

Study
Showing clearly in what order events happen is obviously important, both in narratives and in descriptions of processes such as those in the previous unit. You probably already know how to use certain basic textual connectors such as 'Next', 'Then', 'After that' and so on. In the text of the previous unit and the text you have just read, other ways of showing the order of events can be found.

Answer the following questions about the texts in Units 7 and 8 by referring to an event which is mentioned immediately before the event in question. Also underline the exact words in the texts which give you your answer.
a When are nominations for candidates invited?
b When are the ballot papers printed?
c When are the ballot papers distributed to polling stations?
d When is the elector given a ballot paper?

e When does the elector go to a polling booth?
f When does the elector fold the paper and drop it into a ballot box?
g When did Hardraada's army disembark near York?
h When did Hardraada defeat the northern earls?
i When was Hardraada accepted as king of northern England?
j When was the battle of Stamford Bridge?

From what you have underlined it can be seen that writers can show both the sequence of events and *how long* was the gap in time between one event and another. The different ways of doing this (which you have seen while answering the questions) can be summarized as follows:

1 A simple word or phrase, e.g. 'Then' – useful when the completion of the previous event is already clear and the time-gap is either obvious or unimportant (e.g. last para. text 7).
2 A phrase mentioning a point of time, e.g. 'The day before the election', 'The following day'.
3 A phrase of duration, e.g. 'Four days later'.
4 A phrase stating completion of the previous event, e.g. 'When a date . . . has been fixed', 'having ravaged . . . the . . . coastline' – useful when this previous event is not regarded as being as important as the next one.

Practice

Make the following facts into coherent pieces of writing by using appropriate sequencing techniques.

1 11:02:00 p.m.   moment of earthquake
   11:02:25 p.m.   rumbling noise heard in city
   11:02:35 p.m.   windows begin to rattle
                   loose fittings, ornaments wobble
   11:02:45 p.m.   buildings begin to shake
                   loose fittings, ornaments topple
   11:03:00 p.m.   people begin to run out of buildings
   11:03:05 p.m.   power cut
   11:03:10 p.m.   shaking stops
   11:10:00 p.m.   all roads out of city jammed as people flee city in cars

2 This is a continuation of the text in Unit 7:

polls close 10 p.m. – ballot boxes sealed – taken to central place in constituency – opened – ballot papers counted, a few selected reps. of candidates allowed to observe – number of votes cast for each candidate announced by Returning Officer publicly –

Unit 8

announces name of M.P. for new Parliament – candidate who polled most votes – most urban constituencies can announce result within three hours – by 3 a.m. Friday, more than two-thirds of results declared – if voting very close, candidate may demand a recount – in these cases + some rural constituencies, result not known until well into Friday, even Saturday – but general composition of new Parliament usually already known before that, leader of one party already called to Buckingham Palace and asked to form government.

Textwork

Understanding
Before reading the complete essay, make sure that you know the meaning of these words:

throne	sworn	succession	oath	bowmen
ravage	disembark	earl	rout	cavalry

Now read the text carefully and answer the questions which follow it.

1   When Edward the Confessor died on 5 January 1066 there were two claimants to the English throne. One of these was William, Duke of Normandy. He believed that the throne was rightfully his, both because the King had promised him it and because his main rival, Harold Godwineson, had, he claimed, sworn on the bones of a saint that he would agree to William's succession.

2   But Harold had his own claims. He had been at Edward's deathbed and here the dying King had appeared to confer the kingship on him. Apart from that, he, unlike William, was English and had the support of most of the important people in the country, at least in the south. The day after Edward's death, he was crowned in London.

3   As soon as he heard this news, William sent envoys to Harold to remind him of his oath. Harold bluntly denied William's claims, and the stage was set. By the end of the month, William had begun preparations to take the throne by force of arms. All through the first eight months of that year, while William prepared for war, Harold was working at consolidating his position in the north of the country; and later preparing his own force to meet the inevitable invasion from Normandy.

4   But this was not his only danger. His disaffected brother Tosti had formed an alliance with Harold Hardraada, king of Norway, who also had designs on the English throne. He also had prepared an invasion fleet and on 19 September this fleet, having ravaged much of the north-eastern coastline, disembarked near York. On the next day, the invaders defeated

Unit 8

the northern earls at Fulford Gate. At the same time, Harold left London with an army to repulse them. Four days later, while Harold was still marching north, Hardraada was accepted as king of northern England at York. But his 'reign' proved to be short-lived. The following day the two armies met and engaged in a great battle at Stamford Bridge. The invaders were routed, and Hardraada and Tosti were both killed. The north was safe for Harold.

Meanwhile, through all of this, William's fleet had been waiting for a favourable wind to set sail for England. On 27 September it came. The following day, William's army landed at Pevensey Bay on the south coast of England. It met no opposition. The small force which Harold had left in the south had gone home to collect the harvest. After establishing a small garrison at Pevensey, William moved the main part of his force along the coast and set up camp at Hastings. On the same day, 29 September, Harold received the news that the invaders had landed.

For the next week, while Harold's tired army was marching south, without its bowmen and cavalry, the Norman invaders were consolidating their position on the south coast, ravaging the countryside around Hastings and forcing the inhabitants to leave their homes. Harold reached London on 6 October. He stayed there a week and then set out again, his army slightly larger than the depleted force which had recently marched down from the north. On the evening of 13 October he took up an excellent defensive position on the brow of Senlac Hill, seven miles from Hastings.

Early on the morning of the following day, William moved his army into position, and the battle, which lasted all day, began. Excellent accounts of this can be found elsewhere. Suffice to say that it was fought with extreme ferocity and bravery on both sides and that it could easily have gone either way. But by the end of the day William's victory was total. Harold and all of his most valued fighting men lay dead. The Duke of Normandy was master of England. Two and a half months later, on Christmas Day, he was crowned king at Westminster Abbey in London and a new phase in the history of England had begun.

On what grounds did William of Normandy claim the throne?
On what grounds did Harold Godwineson claim the throne?
To how many groups of people was Harold not completely acceptable as king?
In what part of England is York? Find evidence for your answer in the text.
In what part of England is Hastings? Find evidence for your answer in the text.
William was ready to invade by the beginning of August; why did he not invade until the end of September?
William and his fleet were able to land on the south coast of England without a fight. Why?

65

Unit 8

Vocabulary
1 Explain the meaning of the following phrases from the text:
the stage was set
had designs on the English throne
his reign proved to be short-lived
the depleted force which had recently marched . . . south
it could easily have gone either way
a new phase in the history of England had begun
2 Now find the words in the text which mean:
give/grant/appoint   emphatically defeated
messengers   fortified military camp
making stronger   reduced/weakened
military agreement   top, near the highest point
push back/defeat   it is enough

Connecting past events

Study
1 The following pairs of events are *simultaneous* – they took place at the same time. Study how they are related in the text.

William prepares for war	
Harold works at consolidating in the north	(para. 3)
The invaders defeat the northern earls	
Harold leaves London	(para. 4)
Harold marches north	
Hardraada accepted as king over the north	(para. 4)
(invaders defeat earls, Harold marches north etc.)	
William's fleet waits for a favourable wind	(paras. 4, 5)
Harold's army marches south	
Normans consolidate on the south coast	(para. 6)

2 As you can see, the following patterns have been used:
while [WAS DOING/DID], [WAS DOING/DID]
[DID]. At the same time [DID/WAS DOING]
. . . ([DID] etc.) . . . Meanwhile HAD BEEN [DOING]/HAD [DONE]
Which pattern is most suitable, and which verb forms should be used, on any one occasion, depends on
• the nature of the verb. Do you wish to emphasize completion (Hardraada was accepted) or continuation (Harold was still marching)?

- the relative importance of the event. Are you describing an event which is central to the progress of the narrative (the invaders defeated the northern earls) or a background event (the Normans were consolidating)?

To help you understand these differences in emphasis, try substituting one pattern for another in the same statements. What difference does it seem to make?

3 The following pairs of events are clearly *sequential* – they happened one after the other. Study how they are related to each other in the text.

William reminds Harold of his oath
Harold denies William's claims (para. 3)
Norwegian fleet ravages coastline
Norwegian fleet disembarks at York (para. 4)
William establishes a garrison at Pevensey
William moves his force along the coast (para. 5)
Harold reaches London, stays there
Harold sets out again (para. 6)

4 As you can see, the patterns used for these kinds of events were:
After/before [DOING], [DID]
HAVING [DONE], [DID]
[DID] and then [DID]
[DID]. [DID] (i.e. no connecting construction)

Which pattern to use depends on
- the relative importance of the event, as before. An important event should always be a main part of the sentence.
- how surprising the event is. It is not surprising that Harold should set out again after staying in London; the reader probably knew already that he would do so. But we cannot know what to expect of Harold when William sent him the reminder in the second paragraph. Notice the two different patterns which are used in these two cases.

5 It will help you here to refer again to the section on sequencing earlier in this unit. This is also a good time to refer back to the sections on connecting past events in Units 1 and 5.

Practice

Connect the following sets of events in the most appropriate way.
1 the explorer weathered the storm – he and his ship found shelter at a desert island – he stayed there five days – he set out again.

Unit 8

2   the bank robber got out of his car – he went straight into the house – he had a cup of tea – he collected the money from its hiding place – the police surrounded the house – the robber left the house – the police arrested him.
3   the country gained the lead in computer technology – the country went to war with its neighbour – the government spent all its money on arms – no money for further research in computers – the country lost its lead in the computer field.
4   the Returning Officer asked the candidates to step up on to the platform – he announced the result – Margaret Jones was the new M.P. – she thanked her supporters – she promised to work hard for the good of the constituency – her supporters cheered noisily – it was almost impossible to hear her.
5   people outside in the street starved – the Royal Family lived in extreme luxury – the army remained loyal to the King – the army was defeated in battle – revolution – the Royal Family was thrown out of the palace – the country became a republic – the palace became the Parliament building.
6   the industrial revolution brought many benefits – it also caused great hardship – machines replaced traditional craftsmen in the countryside – tenant farmers were thrown off their land in the interests of modernization – they moved to the cities – they found work – the conditions were terrible.

Extended writing

1   On page 71 is a timetable outlining some of the events which led to the outbreak of the First World War. This involved two opposing groups of the 'Great Powers' (Germany and the Austria-Hungarian Empire on the one side and France, Russia and Britain on the other side). Both groups regarded themselves as having a large influence over south-eastern Europe, where a number of nationalistic movements were growing in strength. Austria-Hungary saw one of these small nations, Serbia, as a particular threat. But members of the other group thought it was important for Serbia to remain free.

All the powers considered themselves bound to honour the various treaties and agreements they had made with each other so that one country's action led to action by another country in a kind of chain reaction. The case of Belgium is an example of this.

Taking your information from the timetable, use the language you have practised in this unit (where appropriate) to write a narrative essay about these events.

Useful words:
assassination murder with political motives
militants people who believe in something so strongly that they feel extreme action is necessary
ultimatum a demand containing a threat
autonomy self-government
mobilize get ready for war
integrity wholeness, indivisibility
2 Write a similar narrative about any other sequence of events in the past which you think are interesting.

Unit 8

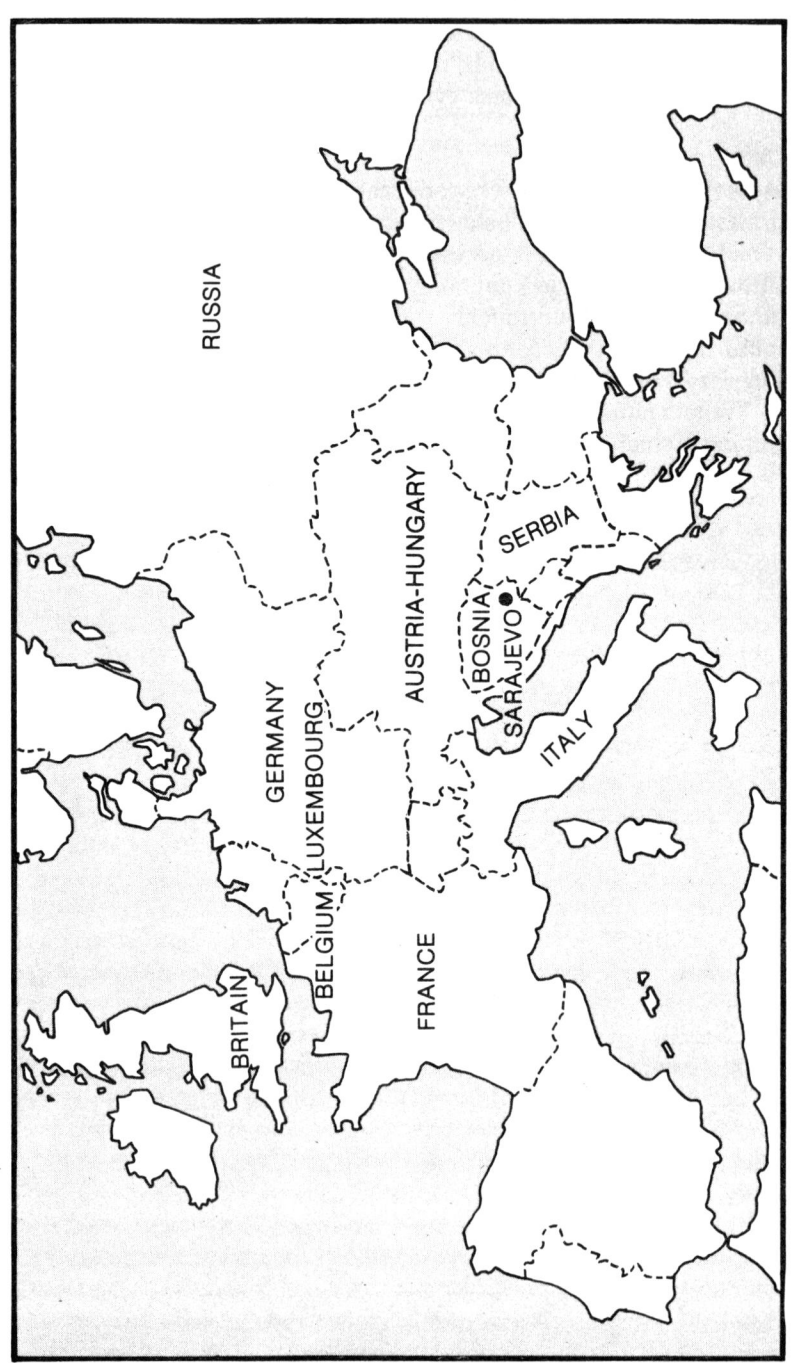

first half of 1914	Opinion grows in Austria-Hungary that Serbia must be attacked Germany, France, Russia increase size of armies
28 June	Archduke Franz Ferdinand of Austria-Hungary assassinated in Bosnia by nationalist militants
early July	Austria-Hungary puts pressure on Serbia, investigates assassination
23 July	Austria-Hungary, with German support, delivers ultimatum to Serbia demanding surrender of Serbian autonomy
26 July	Austria-Hungary rejects moderate Serbian reply
29 July	French government agrees to support Russia to preserve Serbian independence French army takes up defensive positions on border with Germany Austria-Hungary attacks Serbia
30 July	Russia mobilizes
31 July	Britain asks Germany for assurance of Belgium's integrity Germany sends ultimatum to Russia demanding that mobilization stops
1 August	Germany mobilizes, declares war on Russia
2 August	German army moves into Luxembourg
3 August	Britain mobilizes Germany declares war on France
4 August	German army enters Belgium Britain declares war on Germany

Unit 9
Writing information in tabular form

This unit is slightly different. It focuses on two ways of presenting information in tabular form – in a way that is not normal prose – for academic purposes. There is no text; previous texts are used.

Reading Practice
1 Below is a schedule of the Norman invasion. Most of it is incomplete. Complete it by studying the text of Unit 8 and choosing one of the entries from the list below the schedule.

DATES	EVENTS
5 Jan. 1066	Edward dies
6 Jan. 1066	Harold Godwineson crowned king
mid–Jan. 1066	Harold denies William's claims
Feb.–Aug. 1066	
Feb.–Apr. 1066	
Apr.–Aug. 1066	Harold prepares to meet Norman invaders
mid–Sept. 1066	Hardraada and Tosti ravage northern coastline
19 Sept. 1066	
20 Sept. 1066	
24 Sept. 1066	North agrees to Hardraada as king Harold continues march north
25 Sept. 1066	
27 Sept. 1066	
28 Sept. 1066	

29 Sept. 1066	William moves main force along coast to Hastings
29 Sept.–6 Oct. 1066	
6 Oct. 1066	
12 Oct. 1066	Harold sets out with army from London
13 Oct. 1066	
14 Oct. 1066	
25 Dec. 1066	

William lands at Pevensey Bay.
Harold reaches London.
William sends envoys to Harold, reminding him of oath.
Hardraada and Tosti disembark near York.
Battle of Hastings.
William consolidates position on south coast, ravages countryside, forces inhabitants to leave their homes.
Harold routs invaders at Stamford Bridge.
William prepares for war.
Invaders defeat northern earls at Fulford Gate.
Harold consolidates position in north.
William crowned at Westminster Abbey, London.
Harold marches south.
Harold marches north.
William's fleet puts out to sea.
Harold's army moves into position on Senlac Hill.

2 On page 74 is a flow diagram indicating what happens to a ballot paper at a general election. Use the text of Unit 7, and your completion of it in the *Practice* section of *Sequencing* in Unit 8, to complete it. Each box should have an entry.

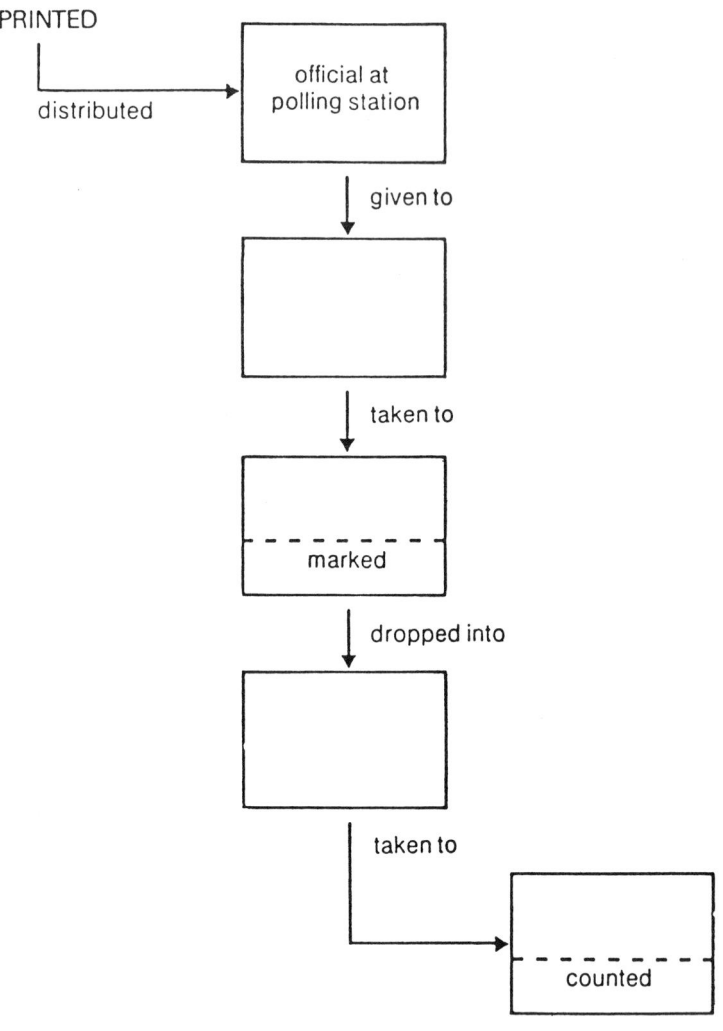

Timetables and schedules

Study
These are useful when accuracy with facts is important and you have to present a large, and possibly confusing number of them in a specific order and with clear time markers. Look carefully at the first page of this unit. The timetable there demonstrates the main

features of this mode of writing. These are:
1 Layout – this can be the same as for plays or transcripts, or, as on the first page of this unit, with lines drawn to mark borders and different sections.
2 Verb forms – what are the words in the timetable which take the place of:
Edward died?
Harold was crowned?
Harold was working at consolidating . . . ?
The invaders defeated the northern earls?
You can see that only two forms are normally used in this type of writing. They are:
[DO/DOES] (in place of active forms).
[DONE] (for passives).
3 Summarizing – what are the words in the completed timetable which take the place of:
a The two armies met and engaged in a great battle at Stamford Bridge. The invaders were routed?
b William moved the main part of his force along the coast and set up camp at Hastings?
c The battle, which lasted all day, began . . . ?
Note the omission of words like 'the', 'a', 'an', 'his', and the general brevity of expression.

Practice
1 Turn the following sentences into language suitable for timetables and schedules.
a An earthquake killed 700 people.
b Relief for the victims of the earthquake was very slow to arrive because all communication to the affected area was cut, but the first emergency supplies managed to get through three days after the quake.
c At three in the afternoon of 14 December 1911, Raoul Amundsen of Norway became the first man in history to reach the South Pole.
d On 16 January 1912, Captain Robert Scott and his party found the tracks which Amundsen had made.
e On 17 January 1912, Captain Scott and his party reached the South Pole, where they found the Norwegian flag flying.
2 Make a schedule of the procedure at a British general election. Use the text of Unit 7, your completion of it in the *Practice* section of *Sequencing* in Unit 8, and the format below.

Unit 9

Election announced   : Nominations invited
Ten days before   :
Nine days before (approx.) :
Day before   :
7 a.m. on day   :
10 p.m.   :
10.05 p.m.   :
10.10 p.m. (approx.)   :
10.45 p.m. (average)   :
1.30 a.m. (average)   : Count finishes
1.35 a.m. (average)   : Result announced

3 Write your own timetable or schedule for any other procedure or series of events with which you are familiar.

Flow diagrams

Study

These are useful when you want to show the movement of something or somebody in a procedure or process. Look carefully at the *Reading practice* about ballot papers in this unit and also the *Extended writing* exercise at the end of Unit 7. Note the following:
- arrows show the progression from one step in the process to the next step.
- alternatives can be shown by having more than one arrow proceeding from a particular step.
- boxes can be used to indicate location, with words added to show what is happening at a particular place.
- times can be added if these are relevant.

Practice

1 A slightly different type of flow diagram can be seen on page 77. It attempts to show the location and movement of the three armies referred to in the text of Unit 8 – Harold's, William's and Hardraada's – over a period of three and a half weeks in 1066. Movement across the page shows the passing of time; movement up and down the page represents the movement of the armies from north to south (although it is not exactly to scale).

In its present form, only the movements of Harold's and Hardraada's armies are shown. Complete the diagram by drawing in lines and names *in the correct places* to show the locations and movements of William's army over the same period of time.

Unit 9

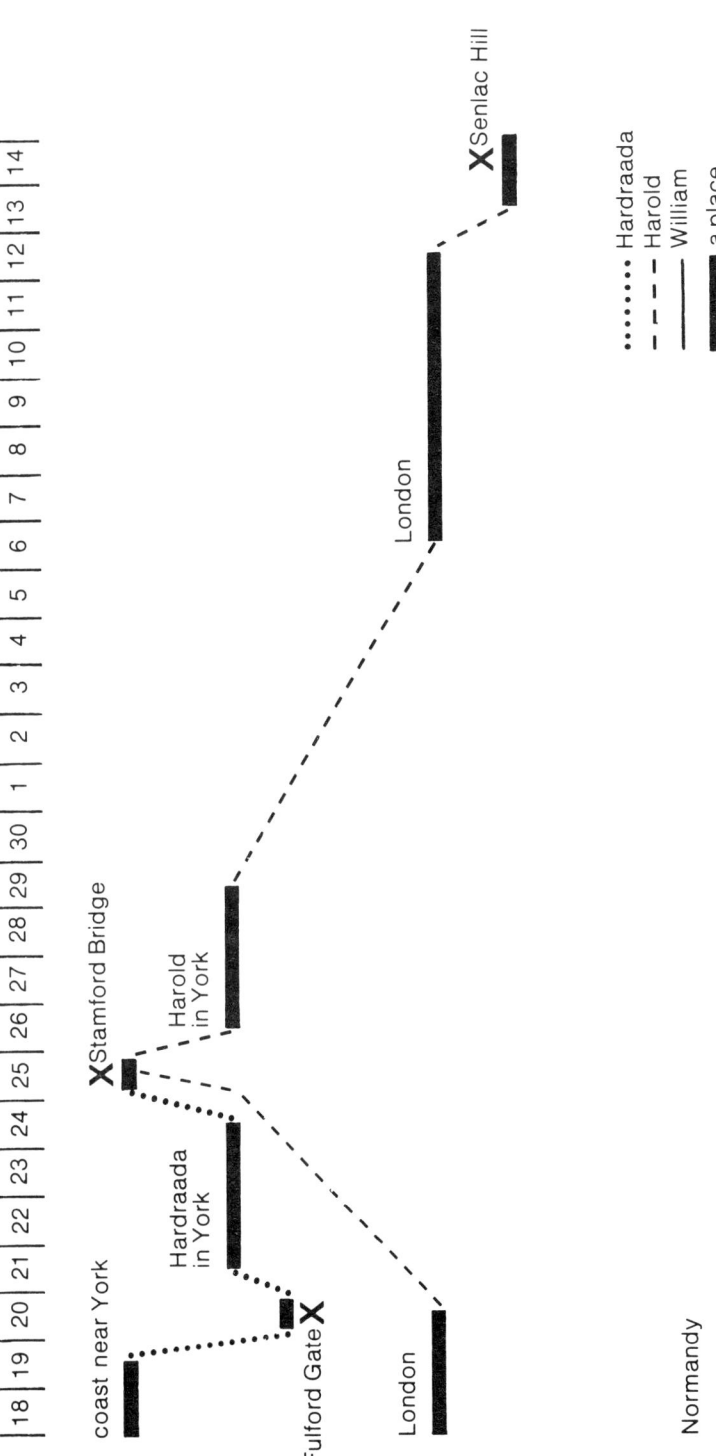

2 Now look back at the *Practice* section of *Impersonal verbal constructions* in Unit 7. Use the notes, or your writing, about the processing of tea to make a flow diagram which shows what happens at each stage.

3 Make a flow diagram for any other process, procedure or series of events with which you are familiar.

Unit 10
Writing advertisements
Classified

Reading practice
A number of extracts from various classified advertisements in newspapers are printed below. First read them and try to decide which ones are advertising:
an object, a job, accommodation for rent, a service.

1 ... Excellent condition ...
2 ... Excellent conditions ...
3 ... No extras ...
4 ... To let ...
5 ... including weekends on a rota basis ...
6 ... £650 o.n.o. ...
7 ... plus bills ...
8 ... Open 7½ days a week ...

Now read the advertisements in full and find whether you were right.

PART TIME HELP required in busy restaurant. Wed.–Fri. 7–12, Sats. all day. Call 333 1048.

£7,000+ Expanding retail business needs energetic sales staff. 5-day week inc. weekends on rota basis. Excellent conditions. Opportunities for overtime and promotion. Phone Jan Smith on 043 672 4949.

PA SECRETARY
PA required, 24–35, for design firm in city centre. Applicants should have good secretarial skills, including shorthand, and be experienced in writing reports and preparing minutes of meetings. A neat professional appearance is essential. Hours and salary negotiable. Please submit CV to Judy Rogers, International Design Group, 6 Burn St, W1.

University of Leicester – Faculty of Law
EUROLEX SCHOLARSHIP
The Faculty of Law and the University Computer Laboratory have entered into a programme of collaboration with EUROLEX in the field of computer-aided legal modelling. Applications are now invited from suitably qualified graduates for a one-year Research Studentship.
The successful applicant, in addition to working with the legal modelling team, will register for a Master's Degree in the Faculty of Law. Applicants should possess a good first degree in Law and should be thoroughly familiar with the law relating to unfair dismissal.
Further particulars may be obtained from the Faculty of Law, The University, Leicester LE1 7RH, where applications (three copies) and a curriculum vitae should be sent, together with the names and addresses of two referees, to arrive not later than 22 August.

Unit 10

5   **VW BEETLE** 1200, 1978 reg., grey, MOT one year, tax October, Motorola push-button radio, front seat covers, new tyres, excellent condition, £650 o.n.o. Tel.: 01 210 4589 (eves., wknds.), 01 358 4320 (day).

6   **HITACHI MICRO RACK SYSTEM,** comprises cassette deck, tuner-amplifier 25 watts, speakers, also turntable. Must sell. £125 o.n.o. Tel.: 6058 9464.

7   **4th person to share.** Own room. £22 p.w. plus bills. Fulton area. Tel.: 45889 eves.

8   **TO LET** Hampstead. Fnshd. hse. btful view. 3 bdrms. 2 recs. lge. k. mod. bth. c.h. £250 p.c.m. Tel.: 01 442 8818.

9   **THE VINE RESTAURANT** 236 High Street, Acton AW3. Tel. 358 0618. Come and enjoy Greek + English cuisine and choose from a comprehensive à la carte menu. Open 7½ days a week, 12 noon – 3 p.m., 6–11 p.m., 11.30 Friday and Saturday. Open Sunday all day.

10 Experienced international removals by road or air. Full service. No extras. Inter-Trans 333 4343.

Textwork

Understanding
Read the advertisements again and then answer the following questions:
Advert. 1   What kind of help is probably wanted?
Advert. 2   Do they want somebody to work at weekends?
Advert. 3   Do you think the job involves dealing with the public? How much money will the successful applicant get?
Advert. 4   How will the person who receives the studentship pay for his/her studies? How can one learn more about the studentship? What is the minimum qualification for applicants?
Advert. 5   How old is the car? Will the buyer have to pay any extra money when he/she buys the car?
Advert. 6   Is it possible that a buyer could buy the system for £100? How do you know?
Advert. 7   Is it the owner or another tenant advertising? What is the rent?
Advert. 8   Is it the owner or another tenant advertising?
Advert. 9   At what hours is the restaurant open on Saturday evening?

Unit 10

Advert. 10 You are going to use the services of Inter-Trans: will the company pack your belongings for you?

Vocabulary
Find the words or phrases in the advertisements which mean:
  we need a part-time helper
  the whole of Saturday
  at least £7,000
  there is a possibility of doing extra work
  you *must* have
  will be agreed by employer and employee
  know (something) very well
  a summary, in tabulated form, of a person's qualifications and career
  or a similar amount
  you would have a room to yourself
  free for somebody to rent
  every month
  any price stated will be the total amount to pay

Abbreviating

Study
Abbreviation is used in many kinds of advertisements. Sometimes it is because space in a newspaper is very expensive; sometimes it is just because the writer is in a hurry.
1 Certain abbreviations have become standard conventions. Learn these:

Abbrev.	Stands for	Means
o.n.o	or nearest offer	perhaps less if nobody will pay as much (as that)
p.w.	per week	every week
p.c.m.	per calendar month	every month
tel.	telephone	phone this number
CV	curriculum vitae	record of someone's work experience and qualifications
a.m.	ante meridiem	from midnight to noon
p.m.	post meridiem	from noon to midnight

81

Unit 10

(Days of the week are abbreviated by using the first letters of the word, e.g. Fri = Friday.)
2 When much abbreviating is done, many types of word are eliminated. These are:

Pronouns (he, she etc.) – see last line, advert. 6.
Verbs (whenever poss.) – see adverts. 5, 10.
Prepositions (of, from etc.) – see first line, advert. 5.
see first line, advert. 6.
Articles (a, the) – see first line, advert. 3.

3 Other forms of abbreviating are a matter of common sense. e.g.
a using a phrase with the verb 'be' whenever possible, and then leaving out the verb. For example, '(The) Salary (is) negotiable' instead of 'The salary can be negotiated with the employer';
b abbreviating words as much as possible. Advert. 8 gives an extreme example of this.

Practice

Abbreviate the following phrases as much as possible (show your effort to another student and see if he/she understands!).
1 . . . you would have your own bedroom but you have to share the kitchen and bathroom . . .
2 . . . the rent is £35 per week. That includes the price of electricity and gas . . .
3 . . . I would like to sell it for about £100 . . .
4 . . . you must be able to provide the names of people who can vouch for your character and ability . . .
5 . . . it has a registration number dating from 1979 . . .
6 . . . a fully furnished flat on the third floor . . .
7 . . . (we) are open from Monday to Saturday . . .
8 . . . furniture which it is very important for me to sell as soon as possible . . .
9 . . . phone 557 0880 in the evenings after half-past six . . .
10 . . . if you want to find out more you can . . .

Careful description

Study
There are conventions governing how to describe what you are offering in an advertisement. It is not common to use words with emotional or subjective suggestions when advertising something for sale, a job or accommodation for rent. In the advertisements in the text you can find

Unit 10

own room	not 'your very own room' or 'lots of privacy'
'excellent condition'	not 'wonderful condition'
'neat professional appearance'	not 'impressive appearance'

On the other hand, advertisements for services, and even advertisements for objects for sale, sometimes exaggerate to make a point. For example, the restaurant in advert. 9 is 'Open 7½ days a week'. The advertiser in advert. 10 might have added a motto like 'We go anywhere'. Literally speaking, both these claims are impossible, but they show people the advertisers' intentions. Readers might be suspicious, however, if the advertiser of advert. 6 had written 'comprises terrific cassette deck, superb tuner-amplifier' etc., even if the deck really is terrific and the tuner-amplifier really is superb!

Practice
Match the following 'flowery' descriptions with the appropriate descriptions below them.
1 possibly a lot more than . . .
2 where you can get your work done without having to do any work at all
3 hardly used (it) at all
4 perfect
5 all the work done for you
  a as new   d top class
  b labour-saving e in excess of
  c full service

Now find more sober descriptions to replace the following expressions:
1 the sort of person who never lets you down
2 free gas, electricity
3 will not only receive lots of money
4 enormous living room
5 the lucky person who gets the job
6 an export company which is getting bigger every day

Extended writing

1 Study the following telephone conversation:

'. . . it's in Handborough, well, not exactly in the town itself but it's only just outside . . . what? . . . oh, yes, it's certainly big enough, two rooms,

Unit 10

and the kitchen's really massive . . . oh, yes, it's all been done up, no problems with things like the cold and that sort of thing . . . no . . . the only thing I'm worried about is . . . well . . . can I afford it? . . . it's £40 a week . . . all in, no bills and things, but all the same it's a bit much . . . er, yes, there *is* somebody underneath, but I met them and they seem quite nice . . . and it's a beautiful old house . . . oh, yes, and those people said I could use the garden whenever I wanted to . . . well, another problem is: what shall I do with my stuff? . . . I mean, I know I haven't got much furniture, but there's certainly no room for it there, and I haven't got anywhere to store it . . .'

Use the conversation to write the advertisement which the speaker originally saw
a in *not more than* thirty words (do not abbreviate words);
b in not more than sixty 'characters' (see page 49). You may have to leave some of the information out to do this. It is possible to leave no space after punctuation marks.

2 Write an advertisement asking for people to act as tourist guides during the summer period. Obviously you want people who can speak at least one foreign language well, if not fluently, and who are generally helpful, friendly and good at dealing with people. The guides have to meet tourists at the airport and see them safely to their hotel, and also to take them on coach tours round the city and to famous places. The money you are offering is quite a lot but you don't offer regular employment, insurance or anything like that. Write the advertisement
a in not more than thirty words;
b in not more than twelve words.

3 Write your own advertisement for something you want to sell. Decide first how much space, or how many words, to allow yourself.

Unit 11
Writing letters of request
Looking for work

Reading practice
1 Read the letter of application for a job, below.
It is a response to one of the advertisements in the text of Unit 10. Which one?
2 The statements below could be used to replace parts of the letter. In each case, decide which phrases could be replaced.
a I am interested in . . .
b I enclose a curriculum vitae.
c I have had a variety of experience in the legal field.
d . . . could you please . . .

Omirou 58
Kolonaki
Athens
Greece

22 July 19. .

Faculty of Law
The University
Leicester LE1 7RH
ENGLAND

Dear Sir/Madam,

 I would like to apply for the Research Studentship which I saw advertised in yesterday's *Times*.
 I am twenty-eight, and have a first-class Honours Degree in Law from the University of Nottingham (1980). Since graduating I have worked in legal practices which specialize in labour relations, in both Greece and Britain. I am particularly interested in the setting up of legal models in a European context and in the application of computer technology in the legal field generally.
 If you think I might be suitable I would be very grateful if you could send me some more information about the Studentship and an application form. I enclose an addressed envelope and an international reply coupon. If you would like to invite me for interview, I will be in Britain from 14 August to 28 August.

 Yours faithfully,

Maria Papadopoulou

Maria Papadopoulou

Unit 11

Textwork

Understanding
Why is the writer writing this letter?
What prompted her to write it?
Does she know exactly who is going to read her letter?
The advertisement in Unit 10 mentions two specific requirements for applicants: does she fulfil these requirements?
Why does she add the sentence about her interests?
What does the writer hope will happen soon?
How has she tried to make this more possible?

Vocabulary
Find the words or phrases in the letter which mean:
   passing final exams at university
   the person you are looking for
   I have put (something) inside the envelope with the letter
   hello
   good-bye

Aspects of letters of request

Study
The following elements often occur in letters which are asking for something:
a a specific request that the reader does something
b a statement of why the letter is being written
c a reference to something the writer has sent with the letter
d information about how (when and where) the writer can be contacted
e information obviously relevant to the subject-matter
f a reference to previous contact between the writer and the reader.

Not all letters of request will have all of these elements. Read the letter in this unit again and
1 decide which of the above elements is *not* included;
2 notice the order in which the other elements appear and in which paragraphs;
3 underline the exact words and phrases which make up elements (a), (b), (c) and (d).

Now look at these extracts from various letters and decide which element is represented in each:

1 Please find enclosed the remittance . . .
2 I am writing to . . .
3 . . . send your full range of . . .
4 . . . at the above address.
5 In your reply you stated that . . .
6 I definitely did not have it with me when I left.
7 You may remember that we . . .
8 I am on holiday until the 15th so . . .

Practice

1   Decide which of the elements identified in the *Study* section are needed in letters to be written for these situations:
a   making a hotel booking
b   after checking out of a hotel you realize that you have left something very important behind
c   responding to an advertisement which offers a free sample
d   someone who owes you money seems to be very slow about paying it
e   you need permission to use somebody's name as a reference.

2   Elements of each of the letters below are in an unsuitable order. Put them in the right order.
a   If you find it, please could you let me know – It is black with one zip compartment and several other compartments. – I think I probably left it somewhere in the reception area as I hurried off for a taxi. – I am writing to you to ask you if you have found a briefcase which I forgot when I left the hotel. – I stayed at the hotel from 25 to 26 January: my room number was 232. – I am afraid it does not have my name on it. – and I will be very happy to claim it. – There were two paperback books and a plastic folder inside it.
b   and would like to apply for the post of trainee sales manager. – Since then I have been working in the dispatch department of a large department store, – I enclose a stamped addressed envelope as requested. – I have got two GCE A-level passes, in mathematics and sociology. – I have seen your advertisement in the *London Herald* of last week. – I can be available for interview at any time. – but I feel I would like to do something more challenging. – If you think I might be suitable, please could you send me some more information about the job? – I am nineteen and left school six months ago.
c   I would be very grateful if this were possible. – I worked for you for about four months in the summer of 1983. – I look forward

to hearing from you. – Recently I have applied for a job with the local council and they have sent me an application form. – I hope you remember me. – They also require the names of three referees. – I am writing to ask you if I could use your name.

Layout and conventions of letter writing

Study
Conventions of letter writing, like fashions, change over the years. The advice below is therefore given in two categories.
1 Some conventions can be regarded as rules – they are unlikely to change, if ever, for a very long time.
a Put your own address, but *not* your name, at the top right of the page.
b Put the recipient's address at the top left (unless it is definitely a personal letter).
c Always remember to date the letter.
d Begin the letter by writing 'Dear . . .'.
e If you do not know the recipient's name or sex write 'Dear Sir/Madam'.
f If you are going to address the recipient by name, write
    Dear Mr Smith   – for a man
    Dear Mrs Smith – for a married woman
    Dear Miss Smith – for an unmarried woman
    Dear Ms Smith   – for a woman whose marital status you do not know, or who you know wishes to be addressed in this way.
g Put this greeting on a separate line and begin the body of the letter below it.
h If you know the name of the person you are writing to, write 'Yours sincerely' on a separate line below the body of the letter; if you do not know the name, write 'Yours faithfully'.
2 There are other conventions that most people, but not everybody, follow at this time:
a Indentation is normally used when writing your address at the top right.
b The recipient's address is usually written *without* indentation against the left-hand margin.
c The date is usually written on the right below the writer's address.
d It is normal to address someone by name whenever this is known.

Unit 11

e People usually sign their name at the bottom of the letter and then print/type their name below that.
f If the letter is not especially formal, and you have had some contact with the recipient before, a more personal greeting is often added before 'Yours sincerely'. This can be 'I (shall) look forward to hearing from you', '(With) Best wishes' or something similar.
g Formal letters are usually as short as possible, provided all the necessary information has been included.

3 The advice above refers mainly to formal letters. Note the following formulas which are often used in informal letters:
a The letter begins with 'Dear (Bob)', but sometimes, if the style is casual and the letter hurried, just '(Bob)'. If the letter is very informal, a term of affection or the word 'Hello/Hi' might be used instead.
b Fairly informal letters can finish with expressions like 'Best wishes', 'All the best' or 'Kind regards'. More casually, the greeting might be just 'Yours'. Very informal letters can, by definition, finish any way you want them to!

Practice
Decide how you would begin and finish letters for the following situations:
1 You have seen an advertisement for a language school in Britain and would like more information.
2 You attended a course at the language school and now you are back in your own country. You would like to attend another course there this summer.
3 You are interested in a job which you have seen advertised. The advertisement says 'Contact Maria Lacey at . . .'.
4 You want to book a room in a hotel.
5 You need a reference from the headmaster of your old school.
6 You decide to write and let your teacher from the language school in Britain know how you are getting on.
7 You are interested in another job. The advertisement asks you to write to 'R. Briggs'.
8 The letter of reply you received about your enquiry for this job was signed 'Rhona Briggs (Miss)'. Now you want to send a covering letter with your completed application form.
9 You want to find out more about a school. The advertisement asks you to write to the headmaster.
10 You are writing to your best friend.

Unit 11

Extended writing

1 Write a letter applying for a job of PA secretary as advertised in the text (No. 3) of Unit 10.
2 Write a letter booking a table at the restaurant advertised in the text (No. 9) of Unit 10.
3 Write a letter to a bank asking for information on taking out a life insurance policy;
    or
write a letter to a language school which you have heard is very good but know nothing about. Enquire whether a course there would be useful for you.

Unit 12
Tabulating biographical information
Curriculum vitae

Reading practice
Here is a curriculum vitae (CV) of someone applying for a job. Before sending it, the writer decided to take a number of statements out of it; these can be found after it. Under which section in the CV would each of them have been put?

Sandra Anne Hodges

Curriculum vitae Born 24/7/55 London

Education
Secondary: Ealing Grammar School, London W5
Tertiary: Pitman Secretarial Training Centre, SW19 (1973-4)
            University of Buckingham (1983-4)

Qualifications
GCE A level: English – Grade B
             Art   – Grade C
RSA Certificate in Secretarial Work (1974)
Honours Degree in Politics, Economics and Law (1984)
Sorbonne Premier (1981)

Employment
1974-6: Typist/clerk, British Market Research Bureau, London W5
1976-7: Audio-secretary, Glacham Pharmaceuticals, Western Avenue, London W13
1977-8: Sales assistant, Hilton Hotel flower shop, London WC1
1979:   Receptionist, small hotel, Paris, France
1980-82: PA secretary, Schwab Beaufort International Ltd, Paris, France: audio-typing, arranging appointments, taking minutes of meetings, writing reports

Other information
Secretary, School Debating Society
Committee Member, Office Workers' Association, Glacham (1977)
University of Buckingham tennis team (1983-4)
Excellent working knowledge of spoken and written French

(1) RSM Certificate in Pianoforte, Grade V (1971).
(2) waitress, Left Bank Bistro, Paris, France (1979).
(3) received tuition in French at private language institute, Paris, France (1980-81).
(4) private tutor in French (1983-4).
(5) voted 'Best-dressed girl' in Glacham office (1977).

Unit 12

Textwork

Understanding
Study the text carefully and answer these questions:
1 About how old was Sandra when she left school?
2 What did she do after leaving school?
3 How old was Sandra when she started university?
4 What did she study there?
5 What experience has Sandra got that is not connected with secretarial work?
6 How many years did she spend outside Britain?
7 Apart from Sandra's claim, what evidence is there in the information to suggest that she knows French very well?
8 Which pieces of information would be interesting to an employer who needs someone who is good at dealing with people?

Vocabulary
Find the words or phrases in the CV which mean:
  any training or education after leaving school
  diploma from a university
  office/organization/company
  exact written records
  reasonable/sufficient/adequate

Special language

Study
With biographical information in tabulated form, the same special features of language are used as with timetables and schedules (see Unit 9). However, in this case the subject is different and the following extra guidelines can be given:
1 Main verbs are hardly ever used. How many can you find in the text here?
2 When verbs are needed, they normally do not need a subject (it is understood to be the writer).
3 Commas are used instead of prepositions (study the information in the last two sections of the text).
4 If the meaning is '(I) was a member of . . .', it need not be stated at all. What was Sandra a member of at the University of Buckingham?

Practice
Turn the following phrases into 'CV language'.
1 Sir Roger Napier was a member of the Royal Horticultural Society from 1954 until his death in 1967. He was Chairman from 1963 until 1965.
2 Charles Dickens was born at Portsea on 7 February 1812 and christened Charles John Huffham.
3 After leaving Acton Comprehensive School I went to Richmond-on-Thames College of Further Education where I stayed, from the autumn of 1979, for two academic years.
4 He was a candidate for the constituency of Billericay in 1955 and again in 1959 before winning a seat at Ealing North at the general election of 1964.
5 I was awarded a degree in geology by the University of Calabria in 1982 and got an M.Sc. in engineering geology from the University of Leeds two years later.
6 After working as a ward orderly at Hounslow Hospital for about six months, I got a job teaching physics, at both O and A levels, at Davies, Laing and Dick Ltd, a private tutorial college in London (W2).
7 While at school I was a member of the football team for two years, being chosen as captain in 1982.
8 At the international symposium about seismology which was held in Athens in 1981 I presented a paper on the effects of earthquakes on wooden structures.

Organizing tabulated information

Study
Look at the text again. Notice that the main organization of the CV is not chronological; it is by categories. Chronology is only used for the ordering inside each category. Note also that:
1 The number of categories and their type can vary according to the person being described. For example, a writer would probably have the category 'Publications'; and you would expect to find the category 'Principal appearances' in biographical details of a famous actor.
2 The most basic, definitive information is written first and the more subjective, anecdotal information afterwards. For example, such things as name, profession and qualifications are given before membership of societies and special, but not 'officially' recognized abilities.

Unit 12

3   Dates are given wherever possible or significant.

Practice
1   Put this police notice in the most suitable order.
Personality: Soft-spoken, but extremely dangerous if annoyed
Height: 1.60 metres
Complexion: Fair
Last seen wearing: Brown anorak, brown casual trousers, brown suede shoes
WANTED in connection with several armed robberies
Hair: Wavy, blond, untidy
Last known whereabouts: Junction of Oxford Street and Charing Cross Road, Sunday, 5 April
CHARLES INNES MacCLENNAN
Build: Stocky, heavy
Distinguishing feature: Extremely heavy, bushy eyebrows
2   Printed below are CV details in the wrong order and without category headings. Organize them properly.

School 1st XV (rugby), 1st XI (cricket)
St Benedict's School, Ealing, London
Working knowledge of spoken French
Sussex University (1977-80)
Edmund Herbert Mallins
William Hill Settling Certificate (1981)
Born 7/9/58
1981-2:   Volunteer work, Angel Park Adventure Playground, London
1981:   Shop manager, Gus Ashe Ltd, SE11
GCE A level: History – Grade A
             English – Grade B
             Maths   – Grade C
Fruit picking, Europe (summer 1981, 1982)
BA Honours degree in social anthropology (1980)
North Lambeth Housing Co-op Committee (1982-3)
1977: Board marker, Ladham's, Hounslow, Middx
1982: Shop manager, Virgil Records, Marble Arch, W1
Secretary, Cowley Estate Tenants' Association, SW9

Some words:
Settling Certificate – a diploma recognizing the holder's ability to compute how much money should be paid to someone who has won a bet

Unit 12

Board marker – a person whose job is to write up the odds being offered on a horse race on a board in a betting shop

Extended writing

1 Use the following transcript of a job interview to write a curriculum vitae for Michael Payne, who was born on 8 February 1958.

Interviewer . . . So you were brought up in Grantham, I see?
Michael Yes . . . well . . .
Int. That's in Lincolnshire, isn't it?
Michael Yes, well, I didn't move there until I was about twelve – my family came down from Edinburgh then . . . That's where they'd always lived . . . but I went to the local grammar school in Grantham.
Int. And when did you come down here to London?
Michael Well, I came down here when I was eighteen to go to art college, as soon as I left . . .
Int. Which college was that?
Michael Chelsea . . .
Int. Oh, yes . . .
Michael and I stayed there for three years, but then I left London again, and, well, I've only actually been based here for six months now.
Int. What brought you back here?
Michael Well, I got married, and my wife has always lived in London and she's got a job here, and so it seemed the obvious place to live.
Int. Have you got a job here already?
Michael Well, I've been doing freelance work, a few shop-fronts, a few one-off contracts with local councils, that sort of thing.
Int. So you've been in the graphic design field ever since you left college?
Michael More or less, though I did get a job as a photographer for a while.
Int. Oh, really?
Michael Yes, with *Britain Illustrated* magazine. I started it in, let's see, it must have been the autumn of '82, but I only stayed there nine months. I found it wasn't quite what I'd expected.
Int. Have you always been interested in photography?
Michael Well, I only became seriously interested as a result of the job I had just before that. I was employed as graphic designer at Snowdonia National Park, doing the signs, and their publicity stuff as well.
Int. And how long were you there?
Michael Well, I went there straight after college, so it must have been from . . . 1979, yes, the autumn of 1979 . . .
Int. And then you got this photography job?

Unit 12

Michael Yes, while I was there, in Snowdonia, there were so many terrific views and that sort of thing that I . . . it encouraged me to take lots of pictures and . . . well, then in 1981 I won an award for one of my pictures, the Charles Spedding Award, and the Park started using some of my pictures on their brochures, so I thought I'd like to try it on a regular basis.

Int. Do you regret having studied graphic design at art college? Rather than something else?

Michael No, not really. I always knew that's what I wanted to concentrate on. In fact I had to fight for it to a certain extent. My parents wanted me to go into accountancy. They thought an A grade A level in maths was more promising than a B grade A level in art, and of course they thought that this kind of life would be much more insecure.

Int. But you haven't found that?

Michael No, I've never been out of work . . . and I think I can hope that I never will be. I got my Higher National Diploma from the college, and it seems to have stood me in good stead.

Int. Have you ever been employed in advertising? I mean with an advertising company like us?

Michael No, my only other period of employment was before I came to London. It was in Manchester, with *Computer Monthly*. I was there for a year.

2 Write your own curriculum vitae.

Unit 13
Describing people
Charles Dickens

Reading practice/Revision
You are going to read an essay on the life, work and character of Charles Dickens, the famous author. Use it to compile biographical data in tabulated form as if it were to be used as an entry in a small encyclopedia.
1 Read the essay, underlining anything which you think is relevant to your encyclopedia entry. Find information on his work and other important things that he did or that happened to him in his life. You should concentrate on 'hard facts' – do not bother with hearsay. As a rough guide, you should expect to underline *no more than half* of the text.
2 Organize your information into suitable categories and write the biographical data in tabulated form, using the techniques you practised in the last unit.

1   Charles Dickens was born at Portsea on 7 February 1812 and christened Charles John Huffham. When he was eleven his father was imprisoned for debt. As there was nowhere else for them to go, his mother and seven brothers and sisters joined their father in prison. Charles was lucky. A kindly relative found him work labelling bottles in a factory.

2   It is hard for us to imagine how the young boy must have felt about these events. It is perhaps difficult to understand the social significance attached to such things in those days. For Charles, it was total shame, and there was his lowly menial job to add to this. The experience of these months (his father was released fairly soon) must have haunted him all his life. John Forster, his closest friend and biographer, tells us that he never told anyone else about it, except his wife.

3   This experience might help to explain the nagging emotional insecurity and restlessness which friends perceived behind the magnetizing eyes, the vivacious personality and, later, the extremely successful author. It might also go some way to explaining Dickens's burning sympathy for the poor and socially oppressed, which is one of the hallmarks of his work.

4   When he was fifteen, Charles began work in a lawyer's office in London. He must have found the nature of the work slow and tedious for, only eighteen months later, he became a freelance reporter. Very quickly, he won himself a high reputation as a reporter of parliamentary debates. His first publication, *Sketches by Boz*, began to appear in magazines when he was still only twenty-one.

5   'The rest', as they say, 'is history'. *The Pickwick Papers* was published in serial form, like all of his novels, over 1836 and 1837. *Oliver Twist* also appeared in 1837. These were followed by *Nicholas Nickleby* in the next two years and *The Old Curiosity Shop* in the two years after that. All were enormous successes.

Unit 13

6   He wrote another ten novels over the following twenty-four years, the most famous of which are *A Christmas Carol* (1843), *David Copperfield* (1849-50) and *Great Expectations* (1860-61). In addition to this he continued to be active in journalism. During the 1850s he contributed regular weekly articles to various publications and was involved with the setting up and editing of a number of his own.

7   What is most impressive about Dickens is his astonishing, apparently limitless energy. When he was not writing he was either travelling (in the early 1840s he went to America, Italy, Switzerland and France), taking part in amateur theatricals both as actor and producer, or, from 1858, giving series after series of readings from his own works. In addition to this he became the father of ten children from his marriage to Catherine Hogarth in 1836.

8   He must have been a tiring, if entertaining, companion. Lionel Trilling wrote that 'the mere record of his conviviality is exhausting'. His biographers suggest he was dedicated to games, fun and almost any kind of celebration with an almost childish intensity. One of his favourite pastimes was taking a very long walk at high speed. He is said to have covered, on foot, every street in every corner of London.

9   In 1866 he travelled to America for the second time for a series of public performances. It is not surprising that by this time his health was beginning to fail. Friends tried to persuade him to slow down, but, perhaps out of a feeling of duty to his public, perhaps simply because of his temperament, he refused to do this. On 8 June 1870 he suffered a stroke after a full day's work and died the following day. So popular had he become that in at least one foreign country, Italy, his death made front-page headlines.

Textwork

Understanding
First make sure that you know these words:
   vivacious   freelance   conviviality   stroke   temperament
Now read the text again and then answer these questions:
1   In what three ways, according to the writer, was Dickens's father's imprisonment significant?
2   What evidence is there in the text to support the writer's contention that Dickens was an unusually energetic person?
3   Does the text suggest that Dickens was, in general, a popular personality as well as a popular writer? Find evidence for your answer.

Vocabulary
1   Explain the following phrases as they appear in the text:

the social significance attached to such things
the magnetizing eyes
go some way to explaining
The rest . . . is history
the mere record of his conviviality is exhausting
2 Now find the words in the text which mean:
given (a) first name(s)
unexciting, with a low social status
disturbed, like a ghost
continual, always not far away, like a toothache
full of life
in a bad position, because of others' behaviour
boring
very strong feeling (here – of enthusiasm)

Degrees of probability

Study
How certain is the writer of the following 'facts' about Charles Dickens:
   his father was imprisoned for debt?
   this experience haunted him all his life?
   he never told anyone about the experience?
   the experience explains his emotional insecurity?
   he was a tiring but entertaining companion?
   he was dedicated to games, fun and celebrations?
   he had walked down every street in London?
   friends tried to persuade him not to work so hard?
   he continued to work as hard as ever?
   he did this because he felt a duty to the public?
You will notice that the writer is not equally certain about all of these things.
1 Some of them are presented as definite facts. If the writer simply states that 'Friends tried to persuade him to slow down' the reader has no alternative but to accept it as true.
2 Some of these statements are reported facts. The writer does not simply state that 'he was dedicated to games, fun and almost any kind of celebration'; he reports other people as stating this. In this way the writer admits the faint possibility that the statement is not 100-per-cent true. The phrases used in the text to show this are, in descending order of probability:

Unit 13

    . . . tells us that . . .
    . . . suggest that . . .
    . . . it is said that . . ./. . . is said to . . .
3 In some of the statements the writer shows that he is only speculating. The phrases used in the text to show this are, in descending order of probability:
    . . . must DO/HAVE DONE
    . . . perhaps . . .
    . . . MIGHT DO/HAVE DONE
Showing clearly your position on the relative truth of a statement is very important in many types of writing if you want to avoid misunderstanding. Here are some more phrases which can be used in this context. Where would you put them on the scale above?
    . . . is believed to . . .   It is probable that . . .
    Some people say that . . .   . . . is unlikely to . . .
    . . . seems to . . .   It is rumoured that . . .

Practice

1 Change each of the following groups of sentences into one sentence without changing the overall meaning. To do this, use one of the phrases above as appropriate.
  a Realizing you are face to face with a murderer is a terrifying experience. It's never happened to me, but that's what I think.
  b Drowning is not at all an unpleasant experience. I wouldn't know; it's never happened to me. But that's what people say.
  c Drowning is not at all an unpleasant experience. That sounds unlikely to me, but I have come across opinions which claim this.
  d Water boils at 100 degrees Celsius. That's what the books tell us, and I don't see how one can possibly disagree.
  e The economic crisis in the last decade made people much more clothes-conscious. I am not 100-per-cent sure about this but I am considering the sales figures for clothes over this period as compared to sales figures for everything else.
  f England is no longer one of the world's most powerful nations. English people are more friendly to foreigners than they used to be. I feel there could be a connection between these two facts.
  g Albert Einstein was not happy at school. He never said this himself. His biographers wrote that.
  h There is a misunderstanding about the settlement of our bill. I think this because you wrote us a cheque for £100. The money you owe us is, in fact, £1,000.

2 Decide what *you* think is the relative truth of the following statements.* Then, in each case, write two sentences, one giving your attitude to the statement and the other supporting your attitude (you can decide which sentence to write first).
a Life 200 years ago was much harder than it is today.
b The invention and use of the atom bomb was a terrible shock to Einstein.
c In the world of science, anything is possible.
d People are less efficient when they work at night.
e Bubonic plague ('the Black Death') was brought to Europe by Marco Polo when he returned from the east.

Point of view

Study
The narratives you read and wrote in the first few units of this book were all written in the first person. There was no obvious difference between the subject of the story (you) and the writer of the story (also you).
The text in this unit is written in the third person. The subject of the text, Charles Dickens, is different from the writer of the text. When writing about anyone else, it is very important to show from which point of view we are seeing things at any one time. Are we seeing things from the point of view of the subject of the text, or are we seeing things from the point of view of the writer or other people? For example, the phrase
'. . . the nagging emotional insecurity and restlessness' (para. 3) tries to show the subject's point of view. The phrase tells us how Dickens *felt*. However, the sentence continues
'. . . the magnetizing eyes, the vivacious personality'.
Here we do not learn anything about Dickens's feelings; we learn about his effect on other people. We are seeing things from other people's point of view.

* NOTES. These facts might help you:
1 Albert Einstein said: 'If I'd known, I would have become a watchmaker.'
2 Arthur C. Clarke wrote: 'If a scientist says that something is possible, he may well be right. If he says that something is impossible, he is almost certainly wrong.'
3 Marco Polo returned from the east in 1295. The Black Death spread over a large part of the world in the fourteenth century.

Unit 13

🔑 Look at the following extracts from the text and decide whether we have been given
a the hero's point of view – how he felt and reacted
or
b another point of view – how the hero looked, seemed and behaved to other people.
1 For Charles, it was total shame . . .
2 The experience of these months must have haunted him all his life.
3 . . . burning sympathy for the poor and socially oppressed . . .
4 He must have found the nature of the work slow and tedious . . .
5 . . . he won himself a high reputation as a reporter of parliamentary debates.
6 He must have been a tiring, if entertaining, companion.
7 . . . the mere record of his conviviality is exhausting . . . any kind of celebration with an almost childish intensity.
8 . . . perhaps out of a feeling of duty to his public . . .

From which point of view we see things is largely a matter of choice of words. It is possible to describe the same feature of a person from either point of view. The sentence at the beginning of paragraph 7:
  'What is most impressive about Dickens is his astonishing, apparently limitless energy'
gives us a picture of Dickens as a phenomenon, a force in the world. By changing the words we use, we can present the same characteristic from the hero's point of view:
  'Dickens could not sit still. He seemed never to feel tired.'

Practice

🔑 1 The following extracts from the text are described from the hero's point of view; they give us an insight into how Dickens felt. With each one, choose the most suitable alternative to the *italicized* words in order to show others' point of view.
a The experience of these months . . . *haunted him* all his life.
  i made him periodically unhappy
  ii echoed in his mind
  iii caused him to be a difficult person to deal with.
b The experience might help to explain the *nagging emotional insecurity* . . .
  i painful self-doubt
  ii continually demanding personality
  iii continual uncertainty and lack of confidence.

c Dickens *had a burning sympathy for* the poor.
   i was a champion of
   ii never forgot
   iii emotionally identified himself with.
d He *found the work slow and tedious* and left to become a freelance reporter.
   i became impatient
   ii was not very successful
   iii was bored to tears with the work.

2 The following piece of writing describes the behaviour of a person in society. It is unsympathetic because it does not try to explain how this person felt at all. Read it, and then rewrite it, using the same details but explaining his behaviour and giving the reader an insight into how he felt. The best way to do this is to pretend that you are the person being described.

> At parties he could be extremely boring. Sometimes he was capable of not uttering a word for hours on end, even if people asked him interesting questions to encourage him. Worse than that, he did not have the grace to understand when his presence was no longer desired. On one of these occasions, when most people had already left, the few people remaining, who were intimate friends, were making it obvious by their unusual silence that it was time for him to go. But he wouldn't. He just sat, completely still, as if he were a stone statue. After hours of tedium and irritation, he suddenly got out of his chair, turned as red as a beetroot, and bolted from the room like a frightened rabbit.

Begin your rewriting like this:

> He found parties a nightmare. The laughter and confident conversation of all the people made him feel so inadequate that . . .

Extended writing

1 Below are a set of notes about the famous explorer James Cook. Use them to write an essay about him. You will have to decide which of the 'facts' below are 'hard facts' and which are only possibly true – use common sense!
Make the description more interesting by describing things from Cook's point of view at suitable places in the biography. The essay will also be more interesting if you show your own reactions to the

Unit 13

facts and what you personally find most interesting about James Cook.

> born 28 October 1728, village in Yorkshire
> father a farm worker
> never saw a book until school
> but very good at arithmetic
> age of twelve, left home to learn shop trade in fishing village
> had never left own village before
> first ever sight of sea from hill overlooking village
> bored by shop work, spent time at waterside
> at fifteen, ran away to sea (trading ship)
> 1755, volunteered for Royal Navy (nobody usually volunteered, life in Navy terrible)
> quick reputation for efficiency
> studied charts and maps
> 1759, sailed ahead making charts for British fleet going to Quebec
> charts perfect, every ship safe
> 1768, first of three famous voyages into unknown seas
> 1776, killed by local people in Hawaii during third voyage
> normally very popular with local peoples
> also popular with crews
> very strict, quiet
> but expert seaman (crew felt safe)
> and concerned for crew's welfare
> (made them eat well, didn't die of scurvy – deaths from scurvy usually commonplace in those days)
> crew refused to leave Hawaii until Cook's body returned
> very enthusiastic to explore
> after second voyage, rich and famous, wife and children in England, further travel unnecessary
> but insisted on going to sea again

2 Write an essay about:
a A person you admire very much
   or
b The most interesting person you have ever met.

Unit 14
More letters of request
Problems

Reading practice
Read the texts of the following four letters and then match them with the addresses of the recipients, which are printed on the next page.

I am writing to ask for your help. I am a teacher of English as a foreign language and am at present engaged in writing a book on writing skills for advanced students, shortly to be published by Penguin.
 I intend to include some material on formal letter writing in the book and naturally I do not wish to find myself in error in the matter of the conventions of such writing.
 Could you possibly advise me on this matter? I would be very grateful if you could do this.

We note that your account No. 45367869 is in debit to the sum of £55.45, and appears to have been so for some time. Please could you advise us as to when you will be able to make up the amount?

I am the tenant of a shop at 4 Wyton Road, Twickenham, known as 'Open Books'. The premises were let by Messrs Burton and White of 18 York Street, Twickenham, and the shop has been open to the public for four weeks.
 During this time, the sign was not removed, and yesterday I telephoned Burton and White to say that it had come loose and I was worried, as there was a strong wind. The neighbouring shopkeepers were also worried, as you can imagine.
 Later during the day the sign fell down. Luckily it injured nobody, as it was hanging over the pavement. However, it tore a large hole in my shop blind.
 I would like to claim for the cost of replacing this blind, which I cannot use while it has a large rent in it.
 I look forward to hearing from you in regard to this matter as soon as possible.

As I have not yet received any reply from you regarding my letter dated 7 July of this year, I will state its main points again.
 The holiday which I booked with your company lived up to none of its promises. We found neither guide nor interpreter at our hotel, which did not have a private beach as the advertisement very clearly claimed. The hotel itself was appallingly dirty and the staff appeared not to have heard of the concept of room service. Coach trips to places of interest in the area never materialized as promised, and we were made to pay for the coach journey to and from the airport.
 If I do not receive a remittance for the amount of my original payment by return, I will be obliged to refer the matter to my solicitor.

Unit 14

D. Bishop Signs Ltd
600 Bishopston Road
Raynes Park
LONDON SW10

Philips Secretarial Training
Queen's Road
LONDON SW19

Supertravel Ltd
47 Grudge Place
LONDON WC3

James O'Driscoll
7 Alton Gardens
LONDON SW19

Textwork

Understanding
Read each of the letters again carefully and then answer the questions.
What, exactly, does each writer want?
Who is the writer of each letter?

Vocabulary
Find the words or phrases in the letters which mean:
soon
have noticed
pay the debt
building, property
ask for money (because it is my right)
which I wrote on
about, on the subject of
money sent by post
inform (somebody so that they can do something)

Different levels of request

Study
The letter in the text of the last unit was a very standard type of request. The letters in this unit are more complicated. In this kind of letter, your tone, and exactly how you make your request, becomes very important.

O—π   Which letter is the most demanding in tone?
Which letter is the most tentative in tone?
Which letter or letters are asking for something which the writer regards as a right?

Which letter or letters are asking for something which the writer regards as a favour?
Which letter is most confident that the request will be granted?
Which letter is least confident that the request will be granted?

Two main elements decide the form a request will take. They are:
- whether, and to what extent, the writer believes he has a right to be granted the request;
- whether, and to what extent, the writer anticipates difficulty in getting the request granted.

Although it would be unlikely that the writer in Letter No. 1 would write 'I am still hoping to receive some advice on this matter' (it might antagonize the reader) or that the writer of Letter No. 4 would write 'Could you possibly send a remittance . . .' (unless he intended to be ironic), the form of the request itself is not the most important aspect of letters of this kind. The important matter is what other elements are there apart from the request itself.

Study the letters again and find out whether the following elements are contained in each case:
- a 'pre-request', a kind of warning that a request is going to be made;
- an argument/explanation immediately after the request about why the writer thinks he has a right to the request;
- a 'pre-thanking' in anticipation of the request being granted;
- a reminder (encouragement) that the writer expects a reply;
- a threat.

Now look back and identify the exact phrases used when these elements are included.

The following general conclusions can now be drawn:
1 If the writer is asking a favour (Letter No. 1) the request is likely to include both a 'pre-request' and a 'pre-thanking'.
2 If the writer is fairly confident, but not certain, of his right to the request (Letter No. 3) the letter will include some explanation/argument of the writer's point of view and a reminder that the writer expects a reply.
3 If the writer is in no doubt about his right to the request or the reader's granting it, no extra elements are needed at all (Letter No. 2).
4 If the writer is in no doubt about his right to the request but is not confident of the reader's granting it (Letter No. 4), a threat may be included.

Unit 14

Practice

1 Decide which of the following elements would be needed in a letter for each situation printed below.
   pre-request
   self-introduction by the writer
   reference to a previous letter
   argument/explanation of the writer's right
   pre-thanking
   reminder that a reply is expected
   threat

a You are thinking of building an extension to your home and want some information from a company which specializes in dealing with such matters.
b You have organized a jumble sale to raise money for a charity and would like a famous TV personality to come and open the sale.
c You need a letter of reference from your previous boss.
d You are the shopkeeper in Letter No. 3 of the text of this unit. The company which put up the sign is refusing to admit responsibility for the damage.
e You believe you are entitled to a rebate on the tax you paid last year.

2 Write out the texts of the following letter-situations from the notes provided.

a You are the shopkeeper in Letter No. 3 of the text of this unit. Your threatening letter was successful and the sign company have agreed to pay, through their insurance company. Now you are writing to the insurance company.
   enclosed, estimate for replacement of blind
   about damage inflicted by . . .
   belonging to . . .
   expect reply soon . . .
   accident occurred three months ago
   if want send someone to inspect, closed Mondays

b You have rented a house belonging to an English family for a summer holiday during the month of August.
   with reference to their previous letter
   happy all arranged
   ask info. *re* what need bring for house (e.g. blankets, cutlery)
   ask advice *re* clothes to bring (never been to Britain before)
   expect reply

c You are writing to your bank manager.

please honour cheque No. 334547
   account No. 44987623
   wrote yesterday
   hospital bill
   will send money (bonus from work) end of month
   Note: honour = agree to pay the amount to the person named
   on the cheque
d You belong to a small firm which makes cabin equipment for aircraft. You are writing to an airline to whom you made a delivery several months ago.
   about our letter of . . .
   no reply
   enclose invoice again
   expect immediate settling of account
   or legal action

Extended writing

1 Some friends of yours from Canada have been staying with you. When you went to the bus station to see them off they had their luggage with them; this included several items of pottery which they had bought while in the country. While at the bus station, a bus ran on to the pavement and crushed their pottery. They were very upset, but they had to leave immediately so as not to miss their plane home.
Write a letter to the Eastern Area Transport Company, 8 Ridge Place, Harford, demanding compensation to be sent to them in Canada.
Do not forget what you have learnt in this and the previous unit. You may also find it helpful to refer back to Unit 4.
2 The following article appeared recently in a local paper.

Plans were announced yesterday by the Ministry of Transport for an extension of the M3 motorway at the London end of its present extent. The extension is to take the motorway through the main street of the busy shopping area of the suburb of Kingley, and also through some of the surrounding residential area, where a number of houses and an old people's home will have to be knocked down and their inhabitants rehoused.
   The plan has caused uproar in local circles. 'What's it going to do to our trade?' said Lionel Brace, a local shopkeeper. 'Nobody likes shopping with all that noise around. And then there's the danger to young children.'

Unit 14

A spokesman for the Ministry of Transport said, 'We are aware that several people will suffer inconvenience, but unfortunately there is no alternative. At present traffic has to detour round by the entrance to the start of the M2, and the congestion there is getting worse every day. Those whose homes are to be demolished will be fully and generously compensated.'

The statement has not impressed local residents. A local Action Group has been formed. One of its members said, 'What has particularly annoyed us was the lack of consultation of local people before the decision was made. Most of us had never heard that a plan like this was in the pipeline. We intend to fight it every inch of the way.'

You are a member of the Action Group. Write a letter to your local M.P. (the Right Hon. Toby Handford, M.P.), stating your case and asking for his support in the matter.

Unit 15
Letters of reply
With regard to . . .

Reading practice
Read the texts of the five letters printed below and decide, as quickly as you can, which involve an element of
a refusal.
b acceptance.
c apology and reassurance.
d anger.

With regard to your application for the above post we regret to inform you that your name was not shortlisted.
Thank you for your interest in the post.

With regard to your letter of 15 April this year, I agree to granting you credit for a deficit of £92.60 as requested and acknowledge your assurance that the amount will be made up at the end of the month.

I have received your statement today for £187.52 and I should like to ask that this be itemized, as I received no invoice with the consignment. I have already remitted a sum of £104.99, which is the total value of the consignment according to the wholesale price list in your catalogue.

Thank you for your letter of 30 May of this year, regarding an unpleasant incident with a member of our staff last week.
I would like to apologize for the long delay at the cheese counter, which was caused by illness among the staff, and the behaviour of the member of the sales staff on duty there, who certainly did not behave with the courtesy expected of our employees.
I cannot, however, agree to your request that the employee in question be dismissed. It was a lapse of which she is not normally guilty, and, in addition, you will appreciate that I am bound by the rules of the Industrial Relations Tribunal in such matters. Please be assured, however, that the employee has been censured and steps taken to ensure that similar occurrences do not take place again.
I hope this has resolved the matter to your satisfaction.

Thank you for your letter of 8 September 1984 in which you referred to our outstanding account with you.
I enclose herewith a remittance for the sum of £43.43 as stated on the account. I apologize for the delay, which was due to a computer error and shortage of staff over the holiday period.
Thank you for your patience.

Textwork

Understanding
To what request was each of the above letters a reply?
(Try to be as detailed as you can.)

Unit 15

Vocabulary
Find the words or phrases in the texts which mean:
  debt
  stated in more detail
  official bill
  delivery of goods
  politeness
  who was concerned in this matter
  I hope you understand/realize
  something (has been) done
  finished/concluded
  not yet paid
  with this letter

Agreeing to and refusing requests

Study
There are two letters at the beginning of this unit which agree to requests. They are Nos. 2 and 5. In both cases we understand that the request has been granted because the writer states what has been done ('I have written your . . . /I enclose herewith . . .'). When granting requests, a statement of action or intended action is all that is usually necessary; but if the request is of a more personal nature, or an invitation, the phrase
  'I will be happy to . . .'
or
  'I will certainly . . .'
often precedes the acceptance.
The same is largely true of refusing requests, but you should also note that:
1 A form of apology is often contained in the statement (Letter No. 1), if it is not already given elsewhere (Letter No. 4).
2 A more impersonal construction (Letter No. 1: '. . . was not shortlisted') can be used where appropriate to make the refusal more emphatic.
3 Look at Letter No. 3, where a refusal is not actually stated. Instead, a point of information is asked for ('. . . this be itemized'). This is useful when you do not want to commit yourself to a definite refusal or agreement. In this letter you can also see a reason for refusing (second sentence), but without the refusal itself; this is another useful way of making your refusal more emphatic.

To summarize, any of the following formulas may be used where appropriate, singly or together:

. . . regret that . . .	(formal)
. . . afraid that . . .	(more personal)
. . . sorry to say that . . .	(even more personal – anxious not to offend)
. . . cannot/will not be able . . .	(personal)
. . . is not/will not be possible . . .	(impersonal, so more emphatic)
(a phrase not mentioning the writer; e.g. Letter No. 1)	(impersonal)
(stating the reason only)	(dismissive, so emphatic)
. . . would like to . . . but (reason)	(personal, not wanting to offend)

Practice

1 Write the one key sentence which would form part of a reply *accepting* the requests in the letters mentioned below.
a – the letter at the beginning of Unit 11.
b – the letter suggested in Unit 11, *Aspects . . . request, Practice 1a*
c – the letter suggested in Unit 11, *Aspects . . . request, Practice 2a*
d – the letter suggested in Unit 11, *Aspects . . . request, Practice 2b*
e – the letter suggested in Unit 11, *Aspects . . . request, Practice 2c*
f – the letter in Unit 14, Text No. 1
g – the letter in Unit 14, Text No. 3
h – the letter in Unit 14, Text No. 4
i – the letter suggested in Unit 14, *Practice 1a*
j – the letter suggested in Unit 14, *Practice 1b*
k – the letter suggested in Unit 14, *Practice 1c*
l – the letter suggested in Unit 14, *Practice 1e*
m – the letter suggested in Unit 14, *Extended writing 2*
n – the letter in this unit, Text No. 4

2 Write one key sentence which would form part of a reply *refusing* the requests mentioned in the letters below.
a – the letter suggested in Unit 11, *Aspects . . . request, Practice 1a*
b – the letter in Unit 14, Text No. 1
c – the letter in Unit 14, Text No. 2
d – the letter in Unit 14, Text No. 3
e – the letter suggested in Unit 14, *Practice 1b*
f – the letter suggested in Unit 14, *Practice 1c*
g – the letter suggested in Unit 14, *Practice 1e*
h – the letter suggested in Unit 14, *Extended writing 2*

Unit 15

Explaining and reassuring

Study
You will notice that Letters Nos. 4 and 5 at the beginning of this unit are longer than the others. This is because the writer of these letters is trying not to offend the reader in any way. Both letters contain:
a reference to the reader's previous letter;
an apology;
an explanation relevant to the reader's complaint;
a final comment designed to 'smooth over troubled waters'.
Note carefully the exact phrases that the writers used to do these things in both cases.
Letter No. 4 is the longer and involves other elements apart from those above. This is because the situation itself is more delicate (dealing with a member of the public, not just an organization, as in Letter No. 5), and is made even more delicate by the fact that the request is being refused. The extra elements are:
an explanation for the refusal (including an appeal to the reader's good sense);
a reassurance that the wrong has been righted.
Note how the writer does these things.

The following phrases may be noted:
Apology:
   . . . apologize for . . .   (standard, formal)
   . . . would like to apologize . . .   ('bigger', formal)
   . . . very sorry about . . .   ('big', informal)
Explanation (*re* complaint):
   . . . , which was due to . . .   (standard, formal)
   (separate sentence)   ('bigger')
Soothing comment:
  Thank you for . . .
  I hope . . .   ('bigger')
  I do hope . . .   ('big', personal)
Appeal to reader's good sense:
   . . . you will appreciate . . .   (standard, formal)
   . . . (as) I am sure you will understand   (more informal)
   . . . (as) you can imagine   (informal)
  I hope you understand . . .   (a little challenging)
Reassurance:
Please be assured . . .   (standard, formal)
I will do my best . . .   (personal)

Unit 15

In especially delicate matters, it is sometimes useful to repeat an apology etc. in a different form.

Practice
Write sentences to form part of a letter, as directed:
1 Apologize for and explain the delay before replying to the writer of the letter in Unit 11, Text.
2 Apologize for and explain your inability to reserve a room for someone at your hotel after you told them over the phone that there would be no problem.
3 Make a soothing comment for situation 2 above.
4 Explain to the writer of the letter in Unit 14, Text No. 1, why you cannot grant his request.
5 Apologize to the writer of the letter in Unit 14, Text No. 3, but explain your refusal to be responsible for the damage.
6 You have agreed to compensate fully the writer of the letter in Unit 14, Text No. 4, and have enclosed the appropriate amount. Now explain why the holiday was such a disaster, as you are very worried that this person might take the matter further (writing to newspapers etc.).
7 Reassure the writer of the same letter.
8 Apologize for the delay in settling an account of £22,000 to a company with which you wish to do business again (so perhaps you should explain as well!).
9 Apologize to your bank manager for your delay in paying back your overdraft of £3.57.
10 You are the M.P. to whom the action group in Unit 14, *Extended writing 2*, wrote asking for support. You are anxious not to make an enemy of the Minister of Transport and so you are sending the group a non-committal reply. However, they are your constituents, and so you do not want to offend them either. Explain to them why you cannot definitely help them (yet) and reassure them of your general support.

Extended writing

1 Write a letter on behalf of the bus company for which you work in reply to the letter in Unit 14, *Extended writing 1*. Use these notes to help you, although you need not follow the order in which the notes appear:
  have sent £68 to friends in Canada

Unit 15

apologize for upset
please understand, station very busy
bus lanes very narrow
have asked for bigger premises
for now, drivers warned of danger
refer to your letter
has not happened before
thanks for bringing this to our attention
do not hesitate to write with further suggestions

2 You recently received the following letter from your bank manager.

We refer you to our letter of 11 July 1985 in which it was noted that your account No. 66685934 was in debit to the amount of £896.42. This is still the case, although when interest is added the amount is very nearly £1,000.

The amount of money which is involved is not small, and the original understanding was that you would have paid off the deficit some six months ago. We would appreciate an immediate deposit to cover the stated amount.

Write a letter in reply, explaining why you cannot comply with the request and asking for the bank manager's understanding as you are going through a difficult period financially. Promise to pay soon.

3 The Home Office in Britain (equivalent to a Ministry of the Interior) has recently sent you a letter demanding your immediate exit from the country, as, according to its records, your permission to stay in Britain expired four months ago. In fact, this is not true; your permit clearly states that you can stay for another five months. Write a short letter of reply.

Unit 16
Letters of information and advice
Britain

Reading practice
You are going to read two extracts (1 and 2) from letters of advice to people who are coming to stay in Britain. Read them and in both cases decide whether the letter is written by:
a an employer to a new employee;
b a university to a new student;
c a family who are going to rent their house to someone they do not know.
d a person to a close friend who is going to visit them in Britain.
Then read them again to find how many of the following topics each letter deals with:
   the British personality
   weather
   entertainment
   transport
   accommodation
   shops.

Extract 1

   We have just received your letter and are glad to learn that all the arrangements are going smoothly.
   Everything you need should be in the house already. There is a full range of utensils in the kitchen, including an electric mixer and a slow-cooking pot, which means that you will be free to explore during the day and still have a meal waiting when you return in the evening. A word of warning: don't bring electric gadgets with you, as the voltage system in Britain is different from everywhere else.
   As far as what clothes to bring are concerned, the weather here in August and September is not as bad as people say. The temperature during the day is usually around 16–22 degrees and sometimes much hotter. But it can get quite chilly at night, so it would be a good idea to bring a pullover and a jacket, but there is certainly no need to bring an overcoat or anything like that. It doesn't usually rain much in these months, but one can never tell – some years we have weeks of glorious weather and some years it rains every other day – so a raincoat would be a good idea . . .

Extract 2

   . . . Britain, like any country, needs a spirit of adaptability by the foreigner. British people may at first seem cold and officious (e.g. when you are going through passport and customs control at Heathrow Airport), but most people are very friendly and anxious to be of assistance after the ice has been broken.

Unit 16

One of the aspects of the country that often poses problems at first is the fact that entertainment events finish early at night. Social gatherings therefore tend to start earlier than in most other countries. In addition shops, although open throughout the day, normally close at 5.30.

Public transport facilities are generally very good but taxis should be avoided, as they are extremely expensive. Car hire terms are fairly reasonable, and second-hand cars can be bought fairly cheaply.

We look forward to seeing you here.

Yours sincerely,

Textwork

Understanding
What is the advantage of using a slow-cooking pot?
Why is it not a good idea to bring electrical gadgets?
Is it normally necessary to wear a jacket during the day?
Why is a raincoat necessary?
What example is given of British 'coldness'?
What aspects of everyday life might seem strange?
What possibilities are there if a visitor to Britain wants to travel a lot?

Vocabulary
Find the words or phrases in the texts which mean:
   makes it possible for you
   You are advised not to
   With regard to (clothes)
   its reputation
   varies between . . . and . . .
   temperatures often fall
   you are advised
   it is not necessary
   Rain is unpredictable
   is recommended

   takes some getting used to
   helpful
   you have got to know them a little
   Perhaps the most difficult thing to get used to
   If you're going to a party, don't forget to go early
   most . . . close at half past five
   don't take

terribly
not very expensive

Informal advice

The people who are corresponding in Extract 1 are not close friends, but the situation is personal and social; the writer is a private individual and the reader is coming for a holiday. The language is therefore fairly informal.

Study
Note exactly how the writer of Extract 1 does these things:
- warns the reader not to bring electrical gadgets
- suggests bringing a pullover and jacket
- says that it is not necessary to bring an overcoat
- suggests bringing a raincoat.

Look also at your answers to the first half of the vocabulary exercise above. These can help you to get the feel of informal ways of presenting information.

Below are a number of ways of advising people in informal situations like that of the first extract.

'weak' advice	– . . . might be an idea . . .
not so weak	– . . . would be a good idea . . .
strong/insistent	– Don't forget/Remember . . .
emphatic	– [DO] . . .
emphatic/insistent	– *Do* [DO] . . .
'weak' negative	– I wouldn't . . .
strong negative	– Don't . . .
unnecessary	– There is no need to . . .
	You don't need to . . . (more informal)

Note also that informal language tends to have the following features:
- personal constructions rather than impersonal ones
('you will be free to explore' rather than 'makes it possible to explore');
- active constructions rather than noun phrases
('not as bad as people say' rather than 'not as bad as its reputation').

Practice
1 Give a piece of informal advice in written form for each of the

Unit 16

following situations, together with the reason for the advice. Use the pattern
   fact 'so' advice
   or
   advice 'as' reason.
a Someone you know is going to spend two weeks in Britain in January when the average temperature is 5 degrees centigrade; but temperatures below zero are not uncommon.
b Someone you know is going to a language school in Britain for the summer. Of course there is the problem of accommodation. Give *two* pieces of advice.
c An old friend of yours has just got a job in the Sultanate of Oman, where it very rarely rains. However, when it does rain there, it rains very heavily, and the result is temporary flooding.
d Someone you know is going to university in America. He/she speaks English well but has always had lessons from British teachers.

2   Extract 1 is the first half of a letter. Write the second half. In this you should:
   warn the reader not to be discouraged by first impressions
   warn him/her about the times of entertainment in Britain and advise them accordingly
   tell him/her about shopping hours
   warn him/her about taking taxis
   suggest hiring a car
   finish with a friendly wish.

Formal advice

In Extract 2 the welfare officer of a university in Britain is writing to a student who is going to attend a course there for three months in the summer. The language here is comparatively formal.

Study
Note carefully how the writer here does the things that you have been told to do in *Practice 2* of *Informal advice* above. Notice that advice is often given by implication only, by statements of what normally happens (e.g. 'Social gatherings . . . tend to start earlier . . .' is advising the reader to make arrangements accordingly). For stronger, more specific advice phrases with
   'should' and 'recommended' or 'you are advised'

are useful. Lack of necessity can be stated by the phrases 'unnecessary' or 'not needed'.
Look also at the answers to the second half of the vocabulary exercise in this Unit to help you get the feel of more formal ways of presenting information. Note that in formal language the following features are predominant:
- impersonal constructions ('when going through . . . customs' for 'when you go through . . .')
- moderate vocabulary ('entertainment events tend to . . . ' for 'everything finishes . . .')

Practice

1   Give a piece of formal written advice for each of the following situations, including a reason for the advice. Use the pattern
   advice 'as' reason
   or
   fact (with advice stated by implication).
a As in *Practice 1a* for *Informal advice,* but this time you are writing on behalf of a government department to several people who are coming on a fact-finding mission.
b As in *Practice 1b* for *Informal advice,* but this time you are writing on behalf of an agency which helps to find people places in language schools in Britain.
c You are writing on behalf of your country's Tourist Board to a group who are particularly interested in archaeological sites.
d You work for a specialist company which gives advice about market opportunities to exporters. You are replying to a company which has asked about selling electric fires in Nigeria.
e This time the company is asking about selling kitchen equipment in Yugoslavia. You do not know whether there are any market opportunities there at the moment. You would only know if you conducted special market research. (Naturally you would be happy to do this, because the company would have to pay you for it!)
2 Write the first half of Extract 2 of the text of this unit. In it you should:
   refer to a previous letter of the reader's;
   explain the university accommodation which she/he will be living in (study-bedroom, share kitchen, bathroom, canteen with meals at all times);
   warn them about electrical appliances;
   tell them about the climate in Britain in the summer; and advise accordingly about clothing.

Unit 16

Extended writing

1 An English family has rented your holiday home in your country and will be arriving on 28 July. They are going to stay six weeks. You have already written to them about what they will find in the house, but you didn't realize that they had never visited your country before. They have written to you asking you for tips about clothing, shopping, travelling inside the country, language problems and if there are any special features of the way of life that they ought to know about.
Write them a letter giving information and advice on these subjects. Their address is 48 The Ridge, Aylesbury, Bucks.
2 Write one of the following letters, giving information and advice as appropriate:
a An English teacher is coming to work at your school and would like to know about general living conditions in your country.
b An English person is coming to work at your company. Write about general living conditions in your country.
c As with *b* above, but this time it is an English doctor coming to work at the same hospital as you.
d You are an expert on your country's economy. Answer an enquiry from a foreign industrialist who is interested in the possibility of opening a large factory making prefabricated parts for the construction industry.

Unit 17
Discussing a phenomenon I
The problem of violence in cities

Reading practice
Printed below is the first part of an essay about violence. Read it as quickly as you can so that you can decide whether the following statements about the writer's opinions are true or false.
1 We cannot decide what to do about the problem of violence until we have decided why it occurs.
2 With a little more effort it would be possible to catch and punish those guilty of violence.
3 People become violent when they know they will not be punished for it.
4 The amount of violence in cities would decrease slightly if people were more prosperous and cities more beautiful.
5 Older cities have fewer problems with violence.

The violence which occurs in situations of extreme political and economic conflict is outside the scope of this essay. I intend to focus on the problem of violence which occurs in otherwise peaceful situations in normal everyday life.

Within these limits the essay title is perfectly right to equate violence with urban life. There is more vandalism, random brutality and murder in cities than there is outside them, and the worst violence often occurs in the largest cities.

It would therefore seem that there is more chance of knowing what to do about the problem if we can learn why this relationship exists. In using this approach I am assuming that the answer to the problem cannot be found simply by making the police more efficient or giving the courts more teeth. Even if all those guilty of violent behaviour could be apprehended and brought to trial (an impossibly expensive proposition in terms of manpower), the imposition of ever harsher penalties does not attack the root of the problem.

Furthermore, this suggested answer is based on the ugly and cynical assumption that people are violent when they have the chance to be. To be sure, human beings are naturally expansive and aggressive, but this is a different matter from the violence which is in question. Apologists for this 'nature red in tooth and claw' point of view fail to see that no species on earth is in the habit of behaving destructively to members of its own kind, or to its environment, without a very clear reason related to its survival. This reason does not apply in the case of urban violence and there is therefore no point in regarding it simply as a natural urge which has to be kept in check.

What, then, are the possible ways in which city life can turn a healthy instinct into a destructive habit? One possibility is frustration and disillusionment. People who come to live in cities do so because they want to get ahead. When their dreams fail to come true they become acutely aware of the inequalities in status and wealth which exist. They find themselves on the lowest rung of the ladder without the beauties of the countryside to console them and without the country's air of stability. The result is an explosion of violence.

6   If this were the case, the solution would seem to be simple, at least in theory; reduce inequality and build beautiful cities.

7   While these improvements would certainly go some way to solving the problem, they do not take into account the fact that useless violence of the kind we are discussing is no greater in cities with extremes of poverty and wealth than it is in the cities of more egalitarian societies. In addition, this disillusionment theory would imply that cities which have been cities for a longer period of time would have fewer problems of violence. In fact, the reverse tends to be true. Cities such as London, where the vast majority of people have been urban dwellers all their lives, suffer far more violence than a city such as Athens, where the majority of the population was born outside the capital . . .

Textwork

Understanding

Printed below is a summary of the essay so far. On the left is a plan of the argumentative movement of the essay; on the right are the arguments themselves. Some of these arguments are missing. Read the essay again carefully, following the movement of the argument, and complete the summary by filling in the missing parts.

Paragraph	Argument
1 limits of topic	– not extreme situations
focus of topic	– 'normal' situations
2 why serious	– more violence in cities
3 procedure	– ask why more in cities
disagree with possible solution	–
reason for disagreeing	–
reason for disagreeing	–
4 further reason for disagreeing	
= disagree with assumption	– people naturally violent
why disagree with assumption	–
5 restate question	–
possible answer	–
6 solution if answer 5 correct	–
7 disagree with solution 6	
= reason	–
reason	– older cities more violent.

Vocabulary
1 Explain the meaning of the following phrases as they appear in the text:
   giving the courts more teeth
   an impossibly expensive proposition
   nature red in tooth and claw
   they want to get ahead
   inequalities in status and wealth
   the lowest rung of the ladder
2 Find the words or phrases in the text which mean:
   range/area
   destruction of, or damage done to, objects
   vicious, violent behaviour (like an animal)
   found and caught
   stricter, more severe
   type of animal
   disappointment due to failure of expectations

Defining the scope of an essay

Study
The theme of the text of this unit is very large (one could write a book about it) and very general. For both these reasons the writer found it necessary to tell the reader clearly what he was going to discuss, and also to remind the reader of his viewpoint and the limits of the discussion.
Answer these questions:
1 What kind of violence does the writer say he is *not* going to discuss?
2 What kind of violence does the writer say he is going to concentrate on?
3 Does the writer say that the essay title is 'perfectly right' to equate cities and violence *in all cases*?
4 What does the writer say he is going to do before discussing possible solutions to the problem of violence in cities?
5 Does the writer think that his approach needs any explanation? What is it?
6 Why, according to the writer, is the fact that human beings are naturally aggressive not relevant to his argument?
7 Why, according to the writer, is the fact that animals behave violently to protect themselves not relevant to his discussion?

Unit 17

8 Does the writer think that the amount of violence is *always* just the same in cities with extremes of wealth and poverty as it is in cities with more social equality?

Note and underline the phrases which helped you to answer these questions.

Here is a list of the things you sometimes have to do when you are writing about serious topics, and some ways of doing them:

State the focus of discussion	– I intend to focus on . . .
	– The biggest problem is . . .
	– The most interesting . . .
State the limits of discussion	– I do not intend to . . .
	– . . . is outside the scope . . .
Remind the reader of the limits of discussion	– the _____ in question
	– in the case of [urban] _____
	– _____ of the kind in question
State your basic assumption and/or viewpoint	– I am assuming that . . .
	– It can be taken for granted . . .

Redefine the topic as your argument progresses.

Which of the questions you answered before referred you to which of these features of defining?

Two of the examples on the right are more informal than the others. Which?

Practice

1 For each of the following essay titles, write at least two sentences explaining exactly what you are going to write about, also making it clear what you are *not* going to write about, and add a basic assumption or viewpoint. The first title has notes to help you.

a The problems facing old people (interested in general social aspects, not in very old, sick, dying; death is inevitable, not a failure).
b The effects of war.
c Dealing with natural disasters.
d The advantages and disadvantages of city life.
e The social value of universities.
f The problems caused by the discovery of nuclear power.

2 The following statements are comments related to each of the essay topics in the exercise above.

Disagree with each of them by writing a sentence which reminds the reader of the limits of your discussion.

a Some old people like to be on their own.

b Many of today's weapons of war eliminate the need for the services of the Red Cross and any other rescue operations.
c Many disasters could be avoided with a little care.
d Despite the great improvements in telecommunications, urban life is still necessary and probably always will be.
e There are a large number of professions which people would probably learn better by receiving training on the job, rather than by going to university.
f There is very little danger of another nuclear bomb ever being dropped.

Analysing opinions

Study
A useful way to show why you disagree with an opinion is to examine the assumptions it is based on. For example, the writer disagrees with the opinion that violence can be stopped by punishing offenders more severely and catching them more often. He produces three reasons to support his argument. The third reason is because he disagrees with something which he thinks the suggestion assumes.
What is the assumption?
How does the writer disagree with it?
Now look carefully at paragraph 7. Here the writer says why he disagrees with the opinion that violence can be stopped by making people richer. He produces two reasons for his disagreement. Both lead the writer to disagree with assumptions he believes the suggestion to carry.
What are the two assumptions?
How does the writer disagree with them?
The following patterns are useful when disagreeing with the basis of an opposite opinion:
. . . based on the assumption/premise that . . . (Disagree)
. . . would imply that/suggest that . . . (Disagree)
. . . does not take into account the fact that (statement which is the opposite from the assumption the writer sees is contained in the suggestion)
. . . ignores the fact that (statement as above)
. . . assumes that . . . (Disagree)

Unit 17

Practice

Disagree with the following opinions by commenting on the assumptions behind them. Use the notes to help you with the first three items.

1 Old people like to have the company of other old people. It would follow that old people's homes are an excellent idea. (Assumption: old people all of one character and one age; but a thirty-year age gap, e.g. between somebody of sixty-five and somebody of ninety-five, very big.)
2 If it is true that practical experience is more valuable than academic knowledge, then universities would seem to be a waste of time. (Assumption: universities exist to train people for jobs.)
3 Now that air travel is available to everybody at a reasonable price it is likely that all other forms of transport over long distances will soon disappear. (Assumptions: nobody finds flying unpleasant; people prefer speed to comfort.)
4 In the nuclear age there is little point in any country maintaining an expensive army and navy.
5 We cannot expect old people to want to live in cities as they find all the noise more unpleasant and the pollution more dangerous to their health than younger people.
6 Unemployed people should not simply be given money by the state. If they want money they should be prepared to work for it.
7 If, as in many countries, the unemployed are given money by the state, they have no right to complain to the state about being unemployed.
8 It is essential that children are made to learn at least one foreign language well. When they grow up it will be too late.

Extended writing

1 Using the language you have practised in this unit (where appropriate) and the notes below,* write an essay discussing 'The value of university education'.

* NOTES.
1 'BUT' signals that the previous statement is being answered.
2 You may reorganize the points if you think it is a good idea.

focus on society, not individual
should it exist?
assume at once it is not for everybody (if it was, would really be secondary education)
shouldn't exist – encourages status society
BUT not the only way to the top
shouldn't exist – practical job training better
BUT need central access to information
BUT modern communications make it unnecessary
BUT not only information important; understanding more important
BUT at work, understanding by example
BUT best at job not always best teachers
should exist – not just for job training
     arts and humanities
    – not just to learn what others know already
     to explore, discover new things
     need university atmosphere for this
     this is major function of university

2 Discuss *one* of the following.
a The problems caused by the increase in terrorism.
b The relationship between sport and international relations.
c the problems of minority communities.

Unit 18
Discussing a phenomenon II
The problem of violence in cities
continued

Reading practice

The second part of the essay on violence is printed below. Read it and then look at the statements printed after it. These are phrases which the writer decided to omit from the final version of the text. Some of them are from the text in this unit and some from the text of the previous unit. Decide exactly where they appeared in the original essay.

8   The problem would therefore seem to be in the nature of city life itself, and in a certain city-bred outlook, rather than in the inability of individuals to adapt to it. It follows that we need to identify those aspects of life which are *inherent* in cities as we know them and which could possibly lead to violence.

9   Mere overcrowding can be immediately dismissed as one of these aspects. It is true that overcrowding beyond a certain extent is known to have disastrous social effects in man as well as in other animals. But these cases are extreme, and most cities do not fall into this category. Before this breaking point is reached, a greater density of population does not seem to lead to greater violence. Again, Athens has a far greater concentration of people living in a limited space than London, and yet is far less violent.

10 However, a universal characteristic of urban life is specialization. All city dwellers play clearly defined and very limited roles in society, and have little first-hand experience of other roles. The worries and details of the lives of others are screened from us in a way that they would not be in rural areas. It is reasonable to suppose that the result of this is, relatively speaking, an inability to sympathize fully with others or to appreciate the value of objects which are not directly connected with our own lives. We do not feel violence done to other people because we cannot understand or identify with the situation of other people. The same is true of damage done to other people's property. This would explain a horrifying phenomenon which is quite definitely unique to city life: the fact that violence can be inflicted on people and objects in broad daylight without anybody attempting to stop it. The city dweller feels unconsciously that experience of life is often the same as the experience of watching a film.

11 Compounding this relative inability to sympathize is the impersonality of city life, where we encounter hundreds of people every day who we do not know in any way at all. In fact, *most* of the people we rub shoulders with are strangers, and we become accustomed to regarding this feature as the norm. Similarly, we are constantly faced with objects which we did not create ourselves, and we have no knowledge of where they came from, who made them, or how they were made.

12 Underlying both of these aspects of city life is the feeling of not being in control of one's surroundings. City dwellers are put in an extremely passive position. Self-expression at all levels is thus extremely limited. It is not stretching a point to see violence as a response to these feelings; as a

perverted outlet for self-expression and a horribly misguided desire to have an effect on one's surroundings, or even simply to get to 'know' people.

1 A city of inhabitants fully accustomed to urban life does not provide immunity from violence.
2 In cities, we live our lives in our own compartments. We occasionally visit a few other compartments, but that is all; and we never stay for long.
3 Cowardly attacks on old people or mindless wrecking of phone booths simply does not have any equivalent existence in the animal world.
4 It seems that we have only a social value but no personal value. This feature of city life is biologically unsuitable to primates such as ourselves; we are not insects.
5 ; we could not have survived as a species without this element in our nature.

Textwork

Understanding
As with the previous unit, complete the framework below:

Para. 8	redefine topic	–
	and, therefore, question	–
Para. 9	disagree with possible answer	– *very* overcrowded
	anticipate objection	= violence; but most cities not like this
	reason for disagreement	–
Para. 10	suggest possible answer	–
	show how it *is* answer	–
	e.g. to support opinion	– violence in broad daylight
Para. 11	suggest further answer	–
Para. 12	result of 10 and 11	–
	show how leads to violence	–

Vocabulary
1 Explain the meaning of these words and phrases as they appear in the text:
   City-bred outlook   this breaking point
   specialization   rub shoulders with
   experience of life is . . . the same . . . watching a film

Unit 18

2 Find the words or phrases in the text which mean:
always/automatically (an aspect of)
personal/direct
shut off, so that we cannot see
not secretly, so that anybody can see
adding to and going together with

Amplifying your argument

Study
It is often not enough simply to state an opinion. This may not be enough to let your readers understand what you really mean, and they may disagree with you because of this. To give your point of view a fair chance it is often necessary to restate it and say more about it.

Look at statements 1–5 after the *Reading practice text* at the beginning of this unit. All of these are examples of this amplification. No. 1, for example, amplifies the opinion

Cities where most people are used to city life have more problems of violence than cities where most people were born outside a city.

Exactly what generalizations in the text do the other statements (2–5) support?

There are other examples of the technique of restating an opinion in the text of this unit. Complete this chart.

Opinion of the characteristics of city life	Restatement of opinion to amplify argument
Para. 10	1 clearly defined roles
	2
	3 screened from other lives
Para. 11 impersonality	1
	2
Para. 12 feeling of not being in control	1
	2 self-expression limited

There are no special phrases or constructions which are particularly useful in this connection. You simply have to do it!

Practice
Explain and amplify each of the opinions below by writing at least two sentences which immediately follow on from the opinion. Where there are notes, use them to help you.

1 One of the major problems of modern life is stress (no time – tied to schedules – high expectations – worried about not achieving).
2 One of the major problems of old people is loneliness.
3 The best doers, or those with the most knowledge, are not necessarily the best teachers.
4 Job training is not the only function of a university.
5 Contrary to popular opinion, learning a language can be easier when you are an adult (know why learning – more powers of analysis – more powers of concentration – can see immediate use).
6 Smoking is anti-social.
7 The anti-smoking and anti-junk-food campaigns being conducted at the moment have unpleasantly religiose connotations (failure if not 100-per-cent fit – morally wrong to be ill – dying as a failure).
8 Bureaucracy is one of the curses of modern life.

Pointing the way

Study
Discussions involve dealing with a large number of ideas which have a varying relationship to each other. Good writing shows clearly what this relationship is and signals the direction of the argument.
The most basic relationship is that of agreement or opposition. You have probably already learnt the use of phrases such as
  Furthermore . . ./In addition . . ./Similarly
which mean:
  'I am going to continue the argument in the same direction.'
There is a new word you have learnt in the *Vocabulary* section of this unit which has the same function.
What is it?
Similarly, you already know the use of 'However' to mean
  'I am going to change the direction of the argument.'
There are other functions which ideas can have in the general trend of the argument. For example, we may wish to agree with an idea but show that it should not be regarded as important.
As well as establishing various combinations of relationship between these ideas, the use of suitable phrases can act as pointers to the reader. They can show which way the argument is going to go and so make it easier to read.

Unit 18

🔑 Six types of these phrases are printed below. Find them in the texts of this unit and Unit 17 and study their use. Then read the list of meanings printed immediately afterwards and match these with the phrases. You may need to use a process of elimination to do this.
1 Even if . . .
2 To be sure . . ./Certainly . . ./It is true that . . ./While . . .
3 One possibility . . ./If this were the case . . .
4 In fact . . . (*two* examples occur in this unit)
5 It is reasonable to suppose . . ./It is not stretching a point . . .
6 . . . this — point of view/theory . . .

a I am going to emphasize a point of view which I have already stated or suggested.
b I realize that the opinion I am about to give might be thought extreme, but I think it is quite logical.
c I am going to give at least two reasons for disagreeing with an idea. The second reason is more important.
d I am going to offer an opinion which I want you to consider, but after that I will probably go on to disagree with it.
e I am referring to an idea which I have already mentioned in a way that suggests I disagree with it.
f I am going to agree *in part* with an idea which I have just mentioned. But after that I will show that my partial agreement is not the important point here.

Practice

🔑 1 Complete the unfinished sentences below in a suitable way.
a I do not agree with the idea that all private transport in cities should be banned. Even if . . .
b I do not agree with the idea that all private transport in cities should be banned. While . . .
c It has been suggested that all private transport in cities should be banned. This autocratic idea . . .
d Banning private transport in cities would do nothing to help people get to work more quickly. In fact . . .
e Banning private transport in cities would not really solve anything. Certainly . . . but . . .
f I can see no value in providing frequent free public transport in cities. As people cannot be persuaded to leave their cars at home under any circumstances, it is not stretching a point . . .
g Something needs to be done about the problem of traffic

congestion in large cities. One possibility . . . However, this idealistic proposal . . .

2 Use suitable phrases from the list in the *Study* section (and others if you find it necessary) to connect each of the following groups of ideas and make a coherent piece of writing.
a disagree that terrorism in recent years has changed nature of society
has deep, terrible effect on those who experience it first-hand
vast majority never have to deal with it
b TV now in every home, children exposed to many harmful influences
idea – ban children from watching too much
idea is tyrannical and based on assumption that children can't make up own minds
children need guidance – this different
idea supposes TV inherently bad
wrong
many educational purposes
c hijacking increasingly widespread problem
idea – arm cabin staff
disagree – not all hijacks could be stopped this way
– danger of accidents in confined space

Extended writing

1 Use the notes below to discuss the proposition that 'Advertising is a waste of time and money'.

First answer – needed to inform; how would people know otherwise?
True that dividing line persuasion/information very thin
but first answer naive
pretends that simple informing is purpose
no – want us to change our minds
also, assumes we *need* to be informed
this doubtful in some cases (example?)
if didn't know, wouldn't be unhappy about not having.
Last point important – advertisers play on feelings of envy.

Second answer – more people buy, product cheaper.
Assumes we *need* to buy:
this true with some products

these cases, only more people buy brand name, not product
also ignores price added to pay for advertising
so no logical reason from society's point of view.
Redefine: whose time? whose money?
Must be worth it to advertisers
plus provides employment
worth it to us if seen as entertainment; some adverts very enjoyable.
(*Conclusion*)

2 Write an essay discussing *one* of the following propositions:
a Television is one of the most potentially dangerous inventions of the twentieth century.
b The motor car is one of the most potentially dangerous inventions of the twentieth century.
c For a child, play is more important than study.

Unit 19
Discussing a phenomenon III
The problem of violence in cities
continued

Reading practice/Summarizing
1 Read the final part of the essay on cities and violence below and summarize the writer's suggestions on what to do about the problem of violence in less than twenty words. Do this as fast as you can.
2 Read the text again and then summarize the writer's suggestions in about 100 words.

If these aspects of life in cities are the answer to why so much more violence exists there than elsewhere, the situation might seem to be hopeless, for they are aspects of life which are absolutely basic to cities as we know them. Wherever there is urban life, there will be violence. Moving people out of old cities and putting them in new ones does nothing to change the situation. The new town of Milton Keynes, about fifty miles north of London, is an example. It was built more or less as a unity, but great care was taken to make sure that the buildings blended with the natural scenery, that all the facilities which people could want were close at hand, and to save the people the danger and unpleasantness of traffic outside their front doors. And yet Milton Keynes has one of the highest incidences of assault and vandalism in Britain.

Why this should be so is not hard to understand. The planners did nothing to disturb the urban pattern of specialization and impersonality leading to frustration which has been identified. Indeed, the feeling of lack of control is probably greater in Milton Keynes than elsewhere precisely because it was planned in such detail, by faceless architects and bureaucrats, and on a very large scale.

The only way we can escape from this vicious circle is if we can create circumstances where people feel more in control of their destinies and freer to organize their lives and surroundings. The appearance of communes is an attempt to create these circumstances. So far, of course, they have had no effect on the amount of violence in cities. There are very few of them and understandably they are based in the country.

They are, however, a step in the right direction in two important ways. First, they are organized on a small scale, and secondly they are organized by individuals rather than an official organization. Both of these features are vital if we want to avoid slipping back into the negative aspects of city life discussed above.

All that can be done by governments is to nudge people gently in the right direction by taking every opportunity to foster a sense of community. If not many opportunities exist, it is all the more important that those that do exist are taken. One of these is to ensure that all public services are organized on the smallest scale possible. Another is to ensure that those guilty of violent behaviour are not further alienated by harsh punishments but encouraged to see themselves as part of the community. Wherever planning of any kind is really necessary, architecture is all-important in

Unit 19

determining whether a community spirit will exist. Evidence that improvements are possible comes from the establishment of a number of neighbourhood councils in inner city areas and from their successful achievements.

18   The significant point about these councils is that they were set up by voluntary action. It should be obvious from the preceding argument that direct action by the state can do little to turn the tide of violence, and indeed sometimes makes it worse. The problem of violence can only be solved by all of *us*. If this seems impractical, and even insulting (why should *I* do anything? – *I'm* not guilty of violence!), it is worth commenting that our immediate assumption that a community problem is something that has to be solved by a government, rather than by the members of the community themselves, is responsible for the feelings of alienation that lead to violence in the first place.

19   The suggestions made above for solving the problem of urban violence are obviously not very spectacular. By their nature they cannot be implemented overnight, since they imply voluntary action on the part of individuals. Nor, when and if these improvements are effected, can a dramatic decrease in the amount of violence be expected. This is because, as was suggested by the comparison of London and Athens, urban violence results from a mental attitude gradually induced by circumstances, and not directly from the circumstances. (This is a further reason why we should not be surprised that Milton Keynes, or any new settlement, is violent; all the inhabitants have come from the city.) It follows that, if the circumstances are changed, the mental attitude of violence will only gradually disappear.

Textwork

Understanding
As before, complete the framework for this part of the essay:
Para. 13   statement of situation   –
           support statement by explanation   –
           support statement by restatement   –
           support statement by example   –
Para. 14   explain situation of example   –
Para. 15   suggest solution   –
           refer to example   –
           limits of example   –
           reason for limits   –
           further reason for limits   –

Para. 16	significance of example	–
	reason for significance	– small scale
	further reason for it	–
Para. 17	suggest further solution	–
	method	–
	method	–
	method	– architecture's role
	support with example	–
Para. 18	warn about nature of solution	–
	anticipate objection	–
	and answer it	–
Para. 19	limit of suggested solutions	–
	second limit of same	– slow change only
	reason for second limit	–

Vocabulary
1 Explain the meaning of these words and phrases as they appear in the text:
   this vicious circle
   neighbourhood councils
   . . . suggestions . . . not very spectacular
   gradually induced by circumstances
2 Now find the words in the text which mean:
   matched, from an aesthetic point of view
   rate of occurrence
   push/encourage (to do)
   encourage/bring up
   made to feel like a stranger

Exemplifying your argument

Study
Another way to make your point of view clearer and stronger is to support a statement with an example. Exemplification can be seen in the text of Unit 17 (the first part of the essay on violence). It works like this:

General statement	**Example**
Cities where people are used to urban life are often more violent than	London
cities where people are new to urban life	Athens

This is a simple example.

Unit 19

○—┐ Now look at the text of this unit to complete the chart below.

General statement	Example	Detail
–	Milton Keynes	–
		but much violence
escape from urban characteristics by creating new circumstances	–	–
		–
improvements are possible	–	–
–	comparison of London/Athens	

When you have completed the chart, look carefully at the text to see how the relationship of generalization to example was indicated by the language.

You will notice that different phrases are used. Which kind of phrase you use depends largely on how much detail you are going to go into with the example. The phrases below are listed in order, with language used for the most detailed example at the top.

_____ is a (very good) example (of this)
_____ is just such a . . .
This can be seen . . .
Evidence . . . comes from . . .
. . , such as _____
(use no special pointers at all)
. . . the comparison of _____ and _____ = parenthetical, a reminder

Note that these patterns do not exclude each other; some of them can be used together.

Practice

○—┐ 1 Below are a number of general statements with examples given in brackets to support them. Using suitable language, connect the examples to the general statements as if they were part of an essay.

a The size of a city is not necessarily a clue to how much pollution it will suffer (London, eight million people, clean – Athens, four million, worst in Europe).

b It is not impossible to overcome problems of pollution in a city,

even when they have become drastic (London, naturally dense atmosphere – coal-burning fires in nineteenth, twentieth centuries – large number of factories – industrial effluent in Thames – 1955, if fell in river, immediately hospital, stomach pump – 1952, 4,000 deaths blamed on smog – 1960s, coal fires banned, factories relocated, heavy fines for dumping in Thames – now, hardly any smog, fish in river, can even swim in it).
c Charles Dickens must have been a very perceptive man who was nevertheless unable to concentrate on any one person or thing for a very long time (characters in books – vivid – accurately reflect habits, mannerisms of time – no depth to them, like cartoons).
d Revolutions, if they are violent, rarely live up to their original high ideals (French – storming of Bastille seen as new dawn for Europe – turned to reign of terror within a few years).
e The geographical size of a country is no indication of its population (Australia – Britain).

2 Support the following general statements with suitable examples:
a The amount of food people eat is not the only determiner of their size.
b How wealthy a nation is is not necessarily a clue to how much political power it has.
c The size of an earthquake is not the only factor which determines how much damage it causes.
d Great authors often become famous *after* their death, but there are some notable exceptions to this.
e *Some* modern buildings are extremely beautiful.

Pointing the way

Study
Below are some more ways of connecting ideas and giving pointers. Notice that many of them are very similar to the phrases in Unit 18, and yet their meanings can be slightly different. Find the phrases in the text of this unit and, where indicated, in the text of Unit 18. Then, as before, match them with the list of meanings printed immediately after them. Do not forget that you may have to do this through a process of elimination.
1 If [DO] . . . (three examples in this unit: compare with 'If [DID]' in Units 17 and 18).

Unit 19

2 . . . , but . . . /And yet . . . (compare with 'however').
3 Indeed . . . (two examples in this unit).
4 The only way . . . /All that can be done . . .
5 Nor . . .
6 It follows that . . . (also in Unit 18).

a I am going to emphasize a point I have just made.
b I am going to change the direction of the argument. The change is not very extreme or significant. I am dealing with a comparatively minor point.
c I am going to make another negative statement.
d I am going to draw a conclusion from what I have just said.
e I am going to suggest a solution to a problem. It is an important solution because it is the only possible one.
f I am going to make a statement and assume it to be true.

A comment is needed on the use of the word *this*. It is used to refer to a topic that has just been mentioned, or that the writer wants us to keep in our minds. Note that
- unlike *the*, it can be used to refer to the whole idea which was expressed in the previous sentence. It is therefore an extremely useful word. Look at its use for this purpose in the 4th sentence in para. 18; the 4th sentence of para. 19; the 5th sentence of para. 19;
- it is used where we would use *that* in the spoken language or in very informal writing.

Practice

 1 Complete the unfinished sentences below in a suitable way:
a Printing vast amounts of paper money does not make a country richer. The only . . .
b Charles Dickens became famous all over Europe. Indeed . . .
c Printing vast amounts of paper money does not make a country richer. Nor . . .
d Printing vast amounts of paper money does not make a country richer. And yet . . .
e If it is true that living in cities demands totally different physical and mental characteristics from living in villages, it follows that . . .
f It seems unlikely that a completely reliable cure for cancer will be found in the next decade. Nor . . .
g It seems unlikely that a completely reliable cure for cancer will

be found in the next decade, but . . .
h Great progress is being made in the treatment of cancer. Indeed
. . .

2 Connect the following sets of statements and make them into a coherent piece of writing by using phrases from the *Study* section of this unit and others where necessary:

a people refuse to leave cars at home
  all attempts to improve public transport system doomed to failure
  relieve traffic congestion, make lights and junctions work as efficiently as possible
b people refuse to leave cars at home
  many people use cars to go round corner only
  traffic congestion relieved when attitudes change
c millions starving
  large numbers of people, more than enough to eat
  looking for new sources of food unnecessary
  trying to turn deserts into fertile land also unnecessary
  also possibly dangerous to climatic balance
  improve communications, encourage fellow-feeling and sympathy.

Extended writing

1 Use the notes below to write an essay on 'Keeping healthy in a polluted world'.

world health improvement in last 100 years
  but signs of increasing twentieth century disease (heart attacks, cancer)
impossible in modern world to be 100-per-cent healthy:
  additives in food
  air pollution
can strike anywhere – oil slick from tanker in 1983, coast of South Africa
  sheep in remote areas affected

possibilities:
don't live in polluted cities – 4,000 deaths London 1952
don't live in cities at all
stress a modern disease
careful with diet

143

Unit 19

    avoid additives in food (can't avoid entirely)
    don't eat tinned food
    try being vegetarian
exercise
    even walking a great help
campaign to make things less polluted
    can't achieve much
    at least shows your attitude

most important: don't worry too much – causes unhappiness this is very unhealthy

2 Write an essay about *one* of the following:
a Feeding the starving millions of the world.
b Easing the traffic problem in big cities.
c The dangers and opportunities of not having to work.

Unit 20
Discussing a phenomenon IV
The instinct for collecting things

Reading practice
In the article you are going to read, the writer offers two possible explanations of why he collects things. Read the article as fast as you can and decide:
1 What are the two possible explanations?
2 Which one does the writer believe is the more important?

I am a compulsive squirrel. I haven't always been that way. At one time I made a point of being as untrammelled as possible. I travelled light. I was as free as the wind. But all that has long since changed. Put me down on Mars now, and in a few years I'll show you a filing problem of DHSS* proportions.

I can't say I get any particular pleasure from all this hoarding. I never sit gloatingly counting my riches. In fact, I see it as a distinct inconvenience. There is nothing image-building or morale-boosting in knowing that you are the proud possessor of several antique plastic cups, large numbers of amorphous pieces of 'ornamentation', and a million pay-slips, bank receipts and bus tickets.

But I am sure I will never throw them out. Every so often I have a blitz. I resolve to perpetrate a night of the large dustbin bags. But it's no good. Forty-eight hours later I have succeeded in liberating myself of a mere fraction of my burden.

After all, who knows, I might need one of those bus tickets one day. It will be my only alibi to clear myself of a charge of mass murder. And who knows, any day now I might get an urge to start a bonsai† vegetable garden, and then my collection of old instant coffee tins will realize their true value.

I try to excuse this idiocy by telling myself that it's all due to my sense of the preciousness of material, my horror at any kind of waste. A tree was cut down to make that bus ticket. Honest toil produced that plastic cup. Am I just going to throw it away? No, I will show my respect, my ecological responsibility. The fact that no amount of bus ticket preservation will bring the tree back, or that bus tickets cannot be recycled, would seem, however, to invalidate this theory.

In reality, my mania is a reaction. When I first started travelling abroad I scorned possessions. In a fit of philosophizing I threw away, gave away or sold almost everything. I have lived to regret bitterly my rashness many times over. When you do not have a settled home the glass jars, bits of paper and all the rest are the only things you have to remind you that you were alive a few years ago. It is difficult to keep in touch with old friends

---
* DHSS = The Department of Health and Social Security: a large government department in Britain.
† Bonsai = The practice of growing plants in miniature, originated in Japan.

when you're thousands of miles apart. It is also difficult to pack chairs and other items of furniture into a suitcase.

7   In a changing world, and especially for someone who moves around a lot, the collection has the enormously valuable function of providing surrogate roots. As such, collecting is not an instinct itself, but rather one possible manifestation of a larger instinct. Whether it is stamps, antique vases or, as in my case, just plain rubbish, it is one of the few things that can effectively provide a sense of continuity.

Textwork

Understanding
Before you read the text again, make sure that you understand these words:
   compulsive   Mars   blitz   roots
Now read the text carefully and answer the following questions:
1 Why does the writer mention the planet Mars?
2 Does the writer enjoy collecting things?
3 What happens when the writer tries to throw things away?
4 Why are mass murder and vegetable gardens mentioned in the text?
5 The writer finds it very difficult to throw anything away: what would he *like* to think is the reason for this?
6 In what sense is this reason illogical?
7 What is the 'larger instinct' referred to in the last paragraph?
8 What two other possibilities does the writer mention for providing a sense of continuity? Why are they not very useful to him?
9 What, in one word, does the writer collect?

Vocabulary
1 Explain the meaning of the following phrases as they appear in the text:
   I'll show you a filing problem of DHSS proportions
   image building or morale boosting
   a night of the large dustbin bags
   my ecological responsibility
   bus tickets cannot be recycled
   a fit of philosophizing
2 Find the words or phrases in the text which mean:
   unfortunately, it is not true (that)   (phrase – para. 2)
   (my attempt) is unsuccessful   (phrase – para. 3)

there is always a possibility (that) (phrase – para. 4)
a strong desire (para. 4)
a mood/period of very strong feeling, like madness (para. 6)
useless things of no value (para. 7)

Using an informal tone

Study
It is not always necessary to be very serious or heavy when discussing a phenomenon. The writer of the text in this unit has significant points to make about what he is discussing, but he uses an informal tone. Doing this can make the discussion more interesting and entertaining. Study the following characteristics of the text:
1 Short sentences.
Look at the first paragraph. How many sentences are there?
2 Informal vocabulary.
Look at your answers to the second exercise in the *Vocabulary* section above. Do they consist of long words or short words?
3 Being personal.
The writer uses his own experience as the basis for the discussion. He also tries to show a personal role in the subject, and tries to involve the reader. Find the phrases in the text which mean:
a Even on Mars a real collector could amass an enormous amount in a few years.
b It should be regarded as a distinct inconvenience.
c . . . in being the proud possessor of . . .
d It is certain . . .
e One possible excuse for this idiocy . . .
f Not having a settled home . . .

Practice
1 Turn the following sets of sentences into informal language, using the characteristics that were noted in the *Study* section above:
a Wasting time is commonly regarded as a negative habit. In fact, the art of being idle happily is a very valuable asset. One useful way of occupying the time is to make lists of tasks that have to be done, although people who compose lists of the different lists that they intend to make can be said to be using this method of passing the time too much.

Unit 20

b The problem of insomnia is one of the most frightening phenomena that many people encounter. Various methods of anaesthetizing the brain, usually involving counting, are commonly employed in an attempt to overcome the problem, but they suffer from the disadvantage that they demand some kind of conscious effort, which is precisely what the sufferer is trying to avoid.

2 Make connected sentences of an informal kind from the following sets of notes:

a Keeping pets:
usually strong opinions, for or against
against – dirty, criminal waste of money
for – really cleaner than human beings, little money, much enjoyment

b The value of the sense of smell:
power of human beings very weak comparatively
advantage – many smells unpleasant
but necessary – awareness of danger
also very evocative of past experiences, memories

Illustrating your statements

Study
Writing is more entertaining, and the points more effective, if opportunities are taken to make it more vivid by using concrete examples of the theme.

1 The theme of the text of this unit is the habit of collecting things. 'Things' is a very vague, abstract word. The writer makes the theme more vivid by constantly referring to particular objects. How many are mentioned in the text?

2 Much of the writer's argument in this case is concerned with showing how ridiculous his collecting habits are. He does this by taking care to refer to obviously useless objects and sometimes placing exaggerated importance on them.
What two reasons are given for the great importance of bus tickets?
Why should a coffee tin not be thrown away?
Why would it be a crime to throw away a plastic cup?

3 The writer also exaggerates in his use of other references. Find the phrases in the text which mean:

a I will have collected so much that finding a place for everything will be a major problem.
b I decide to stay up all night and throw away a very large number of my possessions.
c Because some effort was required to make the plastic cup, I will show my respect for this effort by not throwing it away.

4 A similar effect to exaggeration can be produced by its opposite. This is known as understatement. An example of understatement is referring to the weather as 'rather chilly' when the temperature is 30 degrees below zero, or remarking that lion-taming must be 'not a very healthy pastime' when you mean that it would be extremely dangerous. There is one example of understatement towards the end of the text in this unit. Can you find it?

Practice

1 Write three or four sentences illustrating each of the following statements, using the notes to help you:
a I am always deceived by the names given to colour schemes by paint companies.
  (Mediterranean Blue – will be permanently on holiday)
  (Egyptian Ochre – timeless mystery of the Pharaohs)
  (halfway through doing living room, realize living in the sea is cold, living in a pyramid is boring)
b I like pollution.
  (blast of diesel fumes very warming on a cold winter morning, wakes you up)
  (horns tooting, engines revving outside front door; you know there is life out there – can't get to sleep in perfect silence)
c I can never understand why people are so keen to get money. After all, it has no real value.
  (not nutritious, tasty (sauce?))
  (boring companion, unless . . .)
  (transport?) (comfort?)

2 Write three or four sentences illustrating the following. Remember to use concrete examples and use exaggeration or understatement where appropriate.
a Normally I am fairly moderate about cleanliness. You don't want to live in total squalor, but the odd bit of good clean dirt never hurt anyone. But sometimes I become a fanatic.
b Try as I might, I find it impossible to keep up with the current fashion.

c Illustrate the statements in *Practice 1b* of *Using an informal tone* in this unit.

Extended writing

1 Write an essay about 'Routine', using some or all of the questions below to guide you.
What is your personal attitude to routine? Do you prefer an ordered life or a varied one?
How strongly do you feel about your preference?
Can you think of an imaginary example to illustrate the strength of your preference?
Have you always had this attitude? When did your attitude change, or when was your preference confirmed? What happened?
Are you happy with your present life-style with regard to the question of routine? How would you like to improve it? What happens when you try to change?
Why do you prefer routine/non-routine? What would you particularly dislike about the opposite?
Do you think some or all other people share your preference? What is it about other people (and you?) which makes them feel this way?

2 Write an essay/article about *one* of the following. Use an informal tone and illustrate your point, but remember that you can be as serious or as humorous (or both) as you choose:
a The advantages and disadvantages of being an only child.
b The advantages and disadvantages of coming from a large family.
c Patriotism.
d The desire to achieve status and prestige.

🔑 Key

Notes
1 Note whether the answer you are reading is the *only* answer or a *possible* answer.
2 Remember that if the answer you want is not in the key, it is not important; the important thing was working through the exercise.

Unit 1

Describing decisions – Practice
1a (*possible*) All I could do was to find a café and stay there the night.
 b (*possible*) The only thing to do was to pretend I had done it on purpose and swim to the other side.
 c (*possible*) I thought I could find a taxi, but there were not any taxis either. There was no alternative but to walk.
 d (*possible*) The only thing to do was to start ringing the doorbells of nearby houses and hope someone could give me the shopkeeper's home number. After that I could phone him.
 e (*possible*) There was nothing left to do but to get the vacuum cleaner and suck everything up from the drain. Then I could empty out the dustbag and find it.
With (d) and (e) above, the effort required can be shown more effectively if two sentences are used rather than just one.

Connecting past events – Practice
The answers given are the most suitable, but in many cases not the only possibility.
 1 When I patted the dog, it bit me.
 2 No sooner had I put down the receiver than the phone started ringing again.
 3 John fired the gun and Jack hit the ground like a sack of potatoes.
 4 When I rang the bell the door was opened by a short middle-aged man and I went inside.
 5 As soon as I rang the bell, the door creaked open by itself.
 6 As soon as I opened the door, the full force of the hurricane hit me. ('No sooner' is *wrong*; it suggests surprise at the existence of the hurricane, which would be impossible.)
 7 (It was a very unlucky year for California.) No sooner had the floodwaters abated than an earthquake hit the area.
 8 As soon as the result of the election was beyond doubt, people

Key to Unit 1–2

started celebrating in the streets. ('No sooner' is *wrong* again.)
9 The second they realized they weren't welcome, they left.
10 When he *had* passed through customs, he phoned his girlfriend and she came to meet him.

Unit 2

Giving the background to a story – Practice
1 . . . We *had landed* some time ago and now I *was waiting* for my luggage. We *had been waiting* for half an hour already and I *was getting* impatient. Also I was nervous because I *was breaking* the law. One of my bags *was crammed* with bottles of perfume. I *was going* home for Christmas, and a month before I *had asked* my four sisters and my mother what they wanted. All of them *had said* perfume and I didn't want to disappoint any of them. Another reason for my unease was that if I had any trouble I would miss my train connection, which *was due to leave* in only forty-five minutes.

After another five minutes my luggage appeared and I made ready to go through customs. My apprehension was heightened by the fact that the very last time I *had been travelling* I *had been stopped* and *asked* to open my suitcase.

Explaining why things happened – Study
a Before the explanation/reason – as, it turned out, because.
b Before the result/consequence – thus, so, in this way, as a result, consequently.

Explaining why things happened – Practice
a (*possible*) As there was a large demonstration going on in the centre of town, I got held up in a traffic jam for more than an hour. As a result, I was extremely late for my appointment.
b (*possible*) I got held up in a traffic jam for more than an hour and consequently I was late for my appointment. It turned out there had been a large demonstration in the centre of town.
c (*possible*) I saw two people standing and talking in the middle of the room, so I walked up and introduced myself to the person I thought was the Director. Unfortunately, he was just another employee. The Director was the other one. As a result, our first meeting got off to a bad start, and we still didn't get on well.
d (*possible*) Because I had introduced myself to the wrong person, our first meeting got off to a bad start.

e (*possible*) As the orange trees had been badly damaged by frost in May, there was a shortage of oranges in the shops. As a result, the price was double that of the previous year.

f (*possible*) I couldn't understand why the price of oranges was so high. It turned out that the orange trees had been badly damaged by frost in May and consequently there was a shortage of oranges.

2 (*possible*) I hadn't done any shopping on Tuesday, as I had forgotten that Wednesday was a holiday. Consequently I had no food in the house at all and so I had to eat out that day. As a result, I was virtually penniless by Thursday.

Unit 3

Reading practice

The best, but not the only, paragraph divisions can be made at:
  line 8 (. . . against the police. / And so . . .)
  line 16 (. . . academic record'. / Meanwhile . . .)
  line 20 (. . . reproachfully. / What did he mean? . . .)
The first and third paragraphs are the ones that deal mainly with what happened.

Showing your attitude – Study

1 b

2a The rewritten version shows stronger feeling. The original version wants to entertain the reader.

b The rewritten version is stronger in feeling. The original version tries to be humorous.

Showing your attitude – Practice

a (iii) is the answer. In (i) the word 'sadly' is asking for sympathy, and (ii) does not make the policeman seem hard, as it shows him engaged in reasonable conversation.

b (ii) is the answer because of 'insisted', which is a moderate way of giving an order, and because of 'seemed very worried', which suggests a weak police biting their nails over an unimportant matter.

c (ii) is the answer. (i) is ironic, and (iii) is more interested in the narrative entertainment.

d (ii) is the answer.

e (i) is the only alternative that does not make fun of the police.

Key to Unit 3–4

2a (*possible*) Taking a deep breath and trying not to panic . . .

Commenting on events – Study
The writer is commenting on 'the things my acquittal depended on'. His comment is 'shocking'.

Commenting on events – Practice
1 (*possible*) But what was rather disturbing at the time was the criteria by which I was selected. The interviewer turned out to be an old friend of my father's and we were able to chat about several mutual acquaintances. As far as he was concerned I came from the right background, I was respectable. I might have been very bad at the job, but it wouldn't have made any difference to the interviewer.
2 (*possible*) But what was scandalous was that there seemed to be no official emergency procedures. Nobody with responsibility could be found to give advice on TV or radio. As a result, most people spent the night on the ground floor of blocks of flats or just outside them, which is the most dangerous place to be if there is a danger of an earthquake. If another earthquake had occurred soon afterwards, there might have been thousands of deaths.

Unit 4

Reading practice
'Bureaucats' is the best title. None of the other alternatives covers the theme of the letter, and it is common for newspapers to give humorous titles which work by a play on words.

Being ironic – Practice
1a pleasantly
 b graciously
 c reassuringly
 d obviously
 e helpfully
 f apparently

Anticipating objections to your argument – Practice
1 (*possible*) It was stupid of the nurses to refuse to believe I was not a patient. I can understand that patients cannot always be believed. But surely they could have seen that I was perfectly healthy. Besides, their mistake might have cost someone their life. This is not an exaggeration. The bed they made me get into was the last empty one in the whole hospital.

2 (*possible*) The country is on the brink of disaster. This is not an exaggeration. Studies show that too much unemployment can rip the fabric of society. This situation is a direct result of the government's economic policy. One could argue that it is the result of international factors beyond the government's control. However, these factors were largely the same under the previous government.

Unit 5

Describing feelings and impressions – Study
The other metaphor in para. 3 is '*sprang* to our feet'.
The other simile in para. 4 is 'it seemed as if a hand had passed over the city and extinguished it like a candle'.

Describing feelings and impressions – Practice
1a (iii)   d (v)
 b (ii)   e (iv)
 c (i)   f (vi)
2a (*possible*) It looked as if it had been hit by a bomb.

Connecting past events – Practice
1a I had just got into the bath when the phone rang. ('Was just about to get' is also acceptable.)
 b I was just about to make a phone call when I realized the phone was not connected (or 'was just going to make').
 c I was walking along the street when I heard somebody call me.
 d I had just crossed the road when I heard a voice calling my name from behind me on the other side.
 e I was just going to cross the road when I noticed a car coming along very fast.
 f I had just dropped off to sleep when I was woken by a terrible noise.
 g I was dozing comfortably in front of the TV when I felt everything start to shake.
2a (*possible*) As they came round the last bend Packard was still well in front. Although he was tiring, he still looked a certain winner. But Voicek was gaining ground with every step and the crowd began to roar. For the last twenty metres they were running neck and neck. The crowd had risen to its feet and was shouting as if it had one voice. In the very last second Voicek inched ahead.

Key to Unit 6–7

Unit 6

Reading practice
Headline possibilities are 'Worst Winter Ever', 'Arctic Hits Britain' etc.

Moving from general to particular – Practice
1 Communications in — have been badly affected by the civil war there. There has been no public transport for several days now and the capital city was without telephones for five hours yesterday.
2 Western Renialand is suffering one of its worst droughts this century. There has been no rain for more than a year. The crops failed last year and the signs are that they will fail again. Mass starvation is now a real possibility. International relief organizations are attempting to get supplies through to the afflicted areas.

Unit 7

Using and explaining specialist terms – Study
The following methods were used to help the reader understand the words in the *Vocabulary* section.
constituency – pre-explanation
returns – explanation by context
Returning Officer – pre-explanation
nominations for candidates – explanation by context
ballot papers – post-explanation
political description – post-explanation
polling station – explanation by context
electoral register – explanation by context
polling booth – explanation by context
ballot box – explanation by context

Using and explaining specialist terms – Practice
1a . . . is known as/is called a ballot paper.
  b (*possible*) The voter is given a ballot paper on which to make his choice.
  c . . . is known as/is called a polling station.
  d A polling station is the place where . . .
  f . . . a political description; that is, the name of the party or viewpoint which he or she represents.
2 (*possible*) The game of football is played between two teams of

🔑 Key to Unit 7–8

eleven players each on a rectangular field about 100 metres long. This is known as the pitch. At each end of the pitch there is a goal. This is an archway about 7.5 metres wide and 2.5 metres high. The aim of the game is to score goals by making the ball go in between the posts of the goal . . .

Impersonal verbal constructions – Study
The two other 'active fallacy' verb phrases in the text are 'nominations close' and 'the polls open'.

Impersonal verbal constructions – Practice
(*possible*) Although a lot of tea is drunk in Britain, it is too cold to grow the plant there. It is grown on hillsides in hot countries such as India. Only the top leaves of the plant are picked. Then they are left in the sun to dry. After that, they are put into boxes and shipped to London, where the boxes are bought by tea merchants. Finally, the tea is put into packets or tins and distributed to shops throughout Britain.

Unit 8

Sequencing – Study
Answers to the 'when' questions are as follows:
a When a date for the election has been fixed.
b Ten days before the election.
c The day before the election.
d After he has been ticked off on the electoral register.
e After he has been given a ballot paper.
f After he has voted.
g After he had ravaged much of the north-eastern coastline.
h The day after he had disembarked.
i Four days after he defeated the northern earls.
j The day after he was accepted as king of northern England.
The words to be underlined are:
a (*answer above*)   f Having voted
b then   g having ravaged
c (*answer above*)   h On the next day
d then   i Four days later
e then   j The following day

Connecting past events – Practice
1 (*possible*) Having weathered the storm, the explorer found

shelter for his ship at a desert island. He stayed there for five days and then set out again.

2 (*possible*) The bank robber got out of his car and went straight into the house. After having a cup of tea, he collected the money from its hiding place. Meanwhile, the police had surrounded the house. As soon as the robber left, the police arrested him.

3 (*possible*) Having gained the lead in computer technology, the country went to war with its neighbour. The government then spent all its money on arms. At the same time it invested no money for further research in computers. It had lost its lead in the computer field.

4 (*possible*) After asking the candidates to step up on to the platform, the Returning Officer announced the result. Margaret Jones was the new M.P. While she was thanking her supporters and promising to work hard for the good of the constituency, her supporters cheered so noisily that it was almost impossible to hear her.

🔑 Key to Unit 9

Unit 9

Reading practice

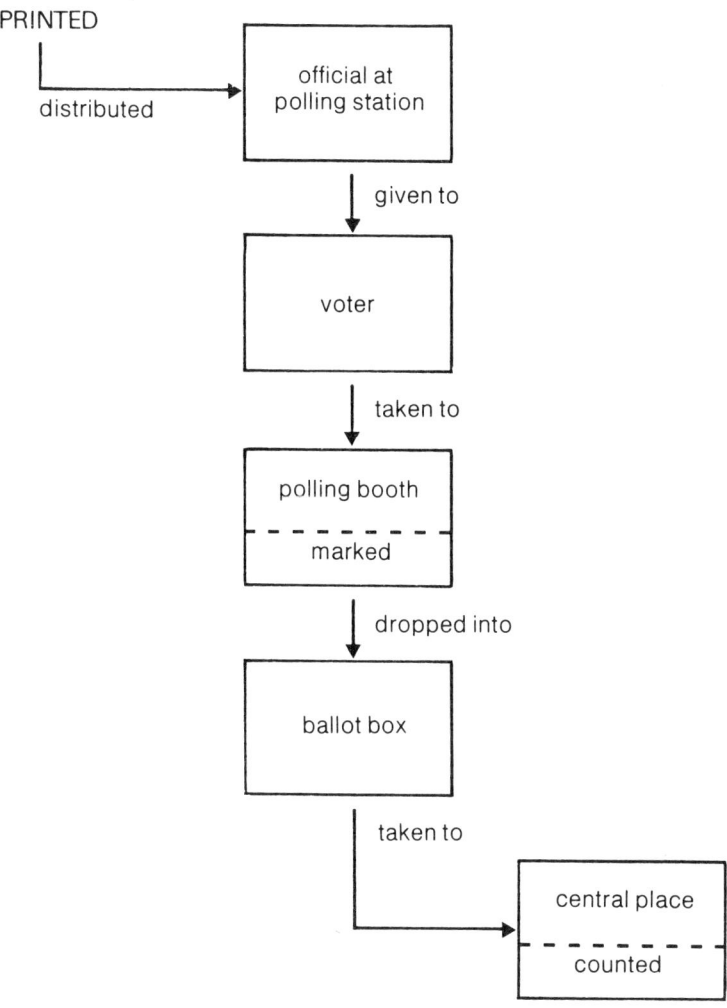

Key to Unit 9

Timetables and schedules – Practice

1a Earthquake kills 700
 b Relief for victims of earthquake slow to arrive (communications cut). First supplies get through three days after.
 c 14 Dec. 1911 3 p.m.: Raoul Amundsen of Norway first man to reach S Pole
 d 16 Jan. 1912: Scott finds Amundsen's tracks
 e 17 Jan. 1912: Scott reaches S Pole, finds Norwegian flag

2 Election announced	: Nominations invited
Ten days before	: Nominations close
Nine days before (approx.)	: Ballot papers printed
Day before	: Ballot papers distributed to polling stations
7 a.m. on day	: Polls open
10 p.m.	: Polls close
10.05 p.m.	: Ballot boxes sealed
10.10 p.m. (approx.)	: Ballot boxes taken to central place in constituency
10.45 p.m. (average)	: Ballot boxes opened, count begins
1.30 a.m. (average)	: Count finishes
1.35 a.m. (average)	: Result announced

Flow diagrams – Practice (see page 161).

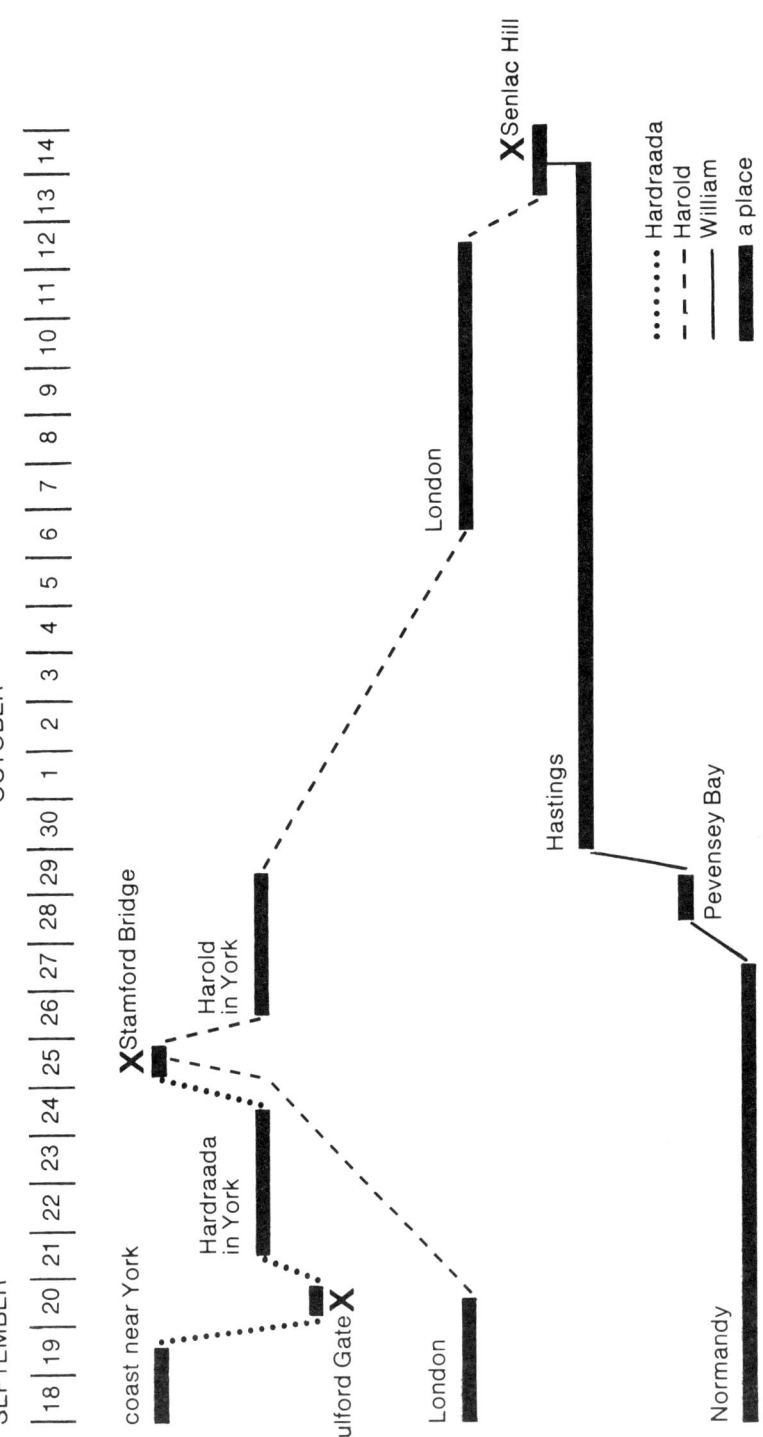

🔑 Key to Unit 10–11

Unit 10

Abbreviating – Practice
In the answers given here, words are not abbreviated unless a standard abbreviation exists, but it would also be possible to abbreviate the words in most cases.
1 . . . own bedroom, share kitchen, bathroom
2 . . . £35 p.w. inc.
3 . . . £100 o.n.o.
4 . . . references essential
5 . . . 1979 reg.
6 . . . 3rd floor, fully furnished
7 . . . open Mon.–Sat.
8 . . . furniture. Must sell.
9 . . . tel. 361 0880 eves.
10 . . . further details/particulars from . . .

Careful description – Practice
1e 2b 3a 4d 5c
1 reliable person/dependable person
2 including . . . /inclusive
3 in addition to a good salary (*possible*)
4 large/spacious living room
5 the successful applicant
6 expanding export company

Extended writing
1a (*possible*) Handborough area. Fully furnished, centrally heated first-floor flat. Two rooms, large kitchen. Beautiful old house with garden. £40 p.w. inclusive. Tel.: 0867 5293
 b (*possible*) Handboro. f. furn. ch. 1st fl. flt. 2r. lge. £40 p.w. inc. 0867 5293

Unit 11

Aspects of letters of request – Study
1c 2b 3a 4d 5f 6e 7f 8d

Aspects of letters of request – Practice
1a (a) is the only essential element.
 b (a),(b),(e) are essential.

🔑 Key to Unit 11–12

c (a) is the only essential element.
d (a),(b),(f) are essential, possibly (e) for persuasion.
e (b),(e),(f) are essential.

Layout and conventions of letter writing – Practice
1 Dear Sir/Madam . . . Yours faithfully
2 Dear [title and name] . . . Yours sincerely (you might also add something like 'I (shall) look forward to hearing from you', depending on the style and size of the school)
3 Dear Ms Lacey . . . Yours sincerely
4 Dear Sir/Madam . . . Yours faithfully
5 Dear Mr _____ . . . I (shall) look forward to hearing from you . . . Yours sincerely
6 Dear _____ (this might be the teacher's first name, or title and surname, depending on the relative formality of the situation) . . . Best wishes . . . (you would either write nothing after 'Best wishes', or something informal such as 'Yours')
7 Dear Sir/Madam (as you do not know the title it is best not to use the name at all) . . . Yours faithfully
8 Dear Miss Briggs . . . Yours sincerely
9 Dear Sir . . . Yours faithfully
10 (Anything you like!)

Unit 12

Reading practice
1 Qualifications
2 Employment
3 Education – Tertiary
4 Employment
5 Other information

Special language – Practice
1 Royal Horticultural Society 1954–67, Chairman 1963–5.
2 Born Charles John Huffham Dickens 7/2/1812 Portsea.
3 Education: Secondary – Acton Comprehensive (197?–9)
            Tertiary – Richmond-on-Thames College of Further Education (1979–81)
4 Candidate Billericay 1955, 1959. Elected Ealing North 1964.
5 Qualifications: B.Sc. geology (Calabria 1982)
            M.Sc. engineering geology (Leeds 1984)
6 Employment: Ward orderly, Hounslow Hospital
            Tutor to A level, Davies, Laing and Dick Ltd, W2

Key to Unit 12–14

7 1st XI football (1981–3), captain (1982–3).
8 Presented paper on effects of earthquakes on wooden structures, International Symposium on Seismology, Athens 1981.

Unit 13

Degrees of probability – Practice
1a Realizing you are face to face with a murderer must be a terrifying experience.
 b It is said that drowning is not at all an unpleasant experience.
 c Some people say that drowning is not at all an unpleasant experience (or 'It is rumoured. . .').
 d Water boils at 100 degrees Celsius.
 e Sales figures for the last decade suggest that the economic crisis made people much more clothes-conscious.
 f Perhaps English people are more friendly to foreigners than they used to be because England is no longer one of the world's most powerful nations.
 g Einstein's biographers tell us that he was not happy at school.
 h There seems to be some misunderstanding about the settlement of our bill.

Point of view – Study
1a 2a 3a 4a 5b 6b 7b 8a

Point of view – Practice
1a (iii) is the answer. The other alternatives describe his feelings ('unhappy' . . . 'in his mind').
 b (ii) is the answer. It describes his effect on other people; the other alternatives describe him worrying about himself.
 c (i) is the answer. It refers to his public role and position; the other alternatives describe his thought processes.
 d (ii) is the answer. The other alternatives describe his feelings.

Unit 14

Different levels of request – Study
Most demanding in tone : 4
Most tentative in tone : 1

Key to Unit 14–15

Writer has a right	: 2, 3, 4
Favour	: 1
Most confident	: 2 (no explanation is required)
Least confident	: 4 (that is why a threat is included)

Different levels of request – Practice

1a *None* of the elements is essential, but self-introduction and pre-thanking are possible.
 b Pre-request, self-introduction, pre-thanking.
 c Pre-request, self-introduction, pre-thanking.
 d Reference to previous letter, explanation of the writer's right, threat.
 e Self-introduction, explanation of the writer's right, reminder that a reply is expected.
2a (*possible*) Please find enclosed an estimate for the replacement of my shop blind, which was damaged by a falling sign belonging to D. Bishop Signs Ltd. I look forward to hearing from you in regard to this matter as soon as possible, as the accident occurred three months ago. If you would like to send a representative to inspect the damage, I would ask you to remember that we are closed on Mondays.

Unit 15

Agreeing to and refusing requests – Practice

1a (*possible*) Please find enclosed an application form and an information sheet about the Studentship.
 b (*possible*) A room has been reserved for you for the night of 17 September.
 c (*possible*) I am happy to inform you that your briefcase has been found.
 d (*possible*) The job involves . . . interview . . .
 e (*possible*) I will be happy to provide a reference.
 f (*possible*) Please find enclosed our Basic Rules booklet.
 g (*possible*) We have instructed our insurance company to pay for the cost of replacement.
 h (*possible*) I enclose herewith a cheque for . . .
 i (*possible*) Please find enclosed our catalogue.
 j (*possible*) I will be delighted to open the sale for you.
 k (*possible*) I hope this testimonial letter is sufficient.
 l (*possible*) Enclosed is a remittance for . . .

Key to Unit 15

m *(possible)* I will certainly do everything I can . . .
2a *(possible)* We regret that the hotel is fully booked until the end of the month.
b *(possible)* Advice of this kind can only be given to people enrolled on one of our courses.
c *(possible)* We should like to ask for details of the extent of the damage.
d *(possible)* We cannot accept responsibility for such matters.
e *(possible)* I would like to come and open the sale but I am afraid I will be working abroad on the date you mentioned.
f *(possible)* It is not the policy of our company to provide references for employees of less than four years' service.
g *(possible)* Our files show that the correct amount of tax was paid by you last financial year.
h *(possible)* I should certainly like to offer my support, but it must be understood that such improvements are very necessary.

Explaining and reassuring – Practice
The following are *possible* answers.
1 I apologize for the delay in replying. Many of our secretarial staff have been away on holiday during the past three weeks.
2 We would like to apologize for our error in giving verbal assurance that a room could be reserved for you. We were at the time collating the bookings which had been received in the previous hour and had no idea that we had received so many. I am sure you will understand that this is a very busy time of year for us and mistakes inevitably occur. (3) I hope this has not inconvenienced you overmuch/caused you great inconvenience.
4 Advice of this kind can only be given to people enrolled on one of our courses.
5 We regret the inconvenience caused to you by the sign. We cannot, however, be responsible for accidents of this kind occurring after a certain/considerable time has elapsed since the installing of the sign.
6 These unfortunate occurrences were due to the fact that our regular agent abroad had recently retired and we seem to have been misled about the credentials of the one we had hired.
7 Please be assured that we were as horrified as you were to learn the truth and have taken every measure possible to prevent a further occurrence of this sort.
8 I should like to apologize for the delay, which was due to an error in our filing system.

9 I apologize for the delay.
10 I will have to see what I can do behind the scenes to improve the situation and indeed to find out if the plans are in their final stage at all. Please be assured that I have every sympathy with you in this matter and will do whatever I can to amend the plans.

Unit 16

Informal advice – Practice
The following are *possible* answers.
1a Sometimes it gets very cold in January, so bring lots of warm clothes.
 b I wouldn't stay in lodgings, as they sometimes make silly rules about what time to be in at night and that sort of thing. The nearby university has halls of residence which will be empty at this time of year, so it might be an idea to find out from the school or the university if you could stay there.
 c There's no need to take things like umbrellas and raincoats, as it hardly ever rains, but when it *does* rain you get flooding for a few days, so it might be an idea to take wellington boots.
 d British and American English are not really very different, but some words for everyday things *are* different, and people's accents will be very hard for you to understand at first; so it would be a good idea to watch as many American films as you can before you go.

Formal advice – Practice
The following are *possible* answers.
a The temperature often drops below freezing point in this month, and warm winter clothing is recommended.
b Most students usually prefer to stay in the halls of residence which the school rents from the university.
c You are advised to plan an itinerary before travelling, as there is an abundance of sites, all of which you may not otherwise have time to visit.
d Temperatures rarely fall below 20 degrees Celsius, and domestic heating of a permanent kind is therefore unnecessary.
e The extent of a possible market in the country is not clear, but preliminary investigations suggest that the prospects are quite good. Detailed market research would be necessary to determine the full situation.

Unit 17

Reading practice
1 True   2 False   3 False   4 True   5 False

Defining the scope of an essay – Study
1 Violence in situations of extreme political or economic conflict.
2 Violence in normal situations.
3 No. Situations mentioned in the first sentence are excluded by the phrase 'Within these limits'.
4 Try to suggest reasons why there is so much violence in cities.
5 Yes. The problem cannot be solved on a merely practical level.
6 Natural aggression is a different thing from what he is discussing.
7 The matter of self-protection has nothing to do with urban violence.
8 No. He reminds the reader that he is only referring to 'useless violence of the kind we are discussing'. Therefore the possibility that violence caused by extremes of poverty, for example, could be greater in such cities is admitted.

Defining the scope of an essay – Practice
The following are *possible* answers.
1a I intend to focus on the social problems of the aged and not on the psychological and physiological problems of the very old, the sick and the dying. I am assuming that death, which is anyway inevitable, should not be regarded as a failure.
 b Economic hardship and chaos, often one of the effects of war, are outside the scope of this essay. I intend to concentrate on the psychological agony and interpersonal problems of the experience of war. It can be taken for granted that war, while it may provide a sense of purpose for the individual at the time, almost always has some lasting negative effect on a person's outlook on life.
2a The social problems of the kind in question do not involve old people's ability or inability to relate as individuals; they involve the problems they have in relating to society at large.
 b The long-term psychological effects in question have no relationship to the availability or non-availability of first aid.

Analysing opinions – Practice
The following are *possible* answers.

1 This convenient idea does not take into account the fact that old people are not all of one character and one age. There is a world of difference between the outlook of a sixty-five-year-old and that of a ninety-five-year-old.
2 This opinion is based on the assumption that universities exist to train people for specific jobs. In fact, most university courses do not have this function.

Unit 18

Amplifying your argument – Study

	Opinion	Restatement to Amplify
Para. 10	specialization	1 clearly defined roles
		2 little experience of other roles
		3 screened from other lives
Para. 11	impersonality	1 most people we meet are strangers
		2 objects also strange to us
Para. 12	no control	1 in passive position
		2 self-expression limited

Amplifying your argument – Practice
1 (*possible*) Not only do we have a sense of time not being our own, of being tied to schedules; we have also been given high expectations and are constantly worried about not achieving our objectives.
2 (*possible*) Most of their friends may have died or be living too far away. In addition, it is very difficult for old people to make new friends, even those of their own age.

Pointing the way – Study
The new word is 'Compounding'.
1c 2f 3d 4a 5b 6e

Pointing the way – Practice
The following are *possible* answers.
1a Even if it could be proved that the measure would make traffic flow better in cities, it would be impossible to enforce.
  b While it is undoubtedly true that something must be done about the problem, this idea is much too extreme.
  c This autocratic idea is merely the pipedream of faceless city planners.

d In fact, it would almost certainly make more people later more often.
e Certainly it would reduce the number of vehicles on the road, but there is no reason to suppose that people would be able to get to their destinations more quickly.
f . . . it is not stretching a point to say that it would make the traffic problem so bad that walking would almost always be quicker.
g One possibility would be to provide free public transport everywhere in the city, so that the number of vehicles on the road would be reduced. However, this idealistic proposal ignores the fact that people will always use their cars if they have any kind of choice.
2a It is a fallacy to claim that terrorism in recent years has changed the nature of society. Certainly it has a deep and terrible effect on those who experience it first-hand, but the fact remains that the vast majority of us never have to deal with it.

Unit 19

Exemplifying your argument – Study

General statement	Example	Detail
making new cities doesn't help	Milton Keynes	great care with planning but much violence
escape from urban characteristics by creating new circumstances	communes	no effect as yet very few, in country
improvements are possible	neighbourhood councils	successful achievements
violence caused by gradual change of attitude	comparison of London/Athens	

Exemplifying your argument – Practice
The following are *possible* answers.
1a London, for example, is relatively free of pollution, while Athens, with half the population of London, suffers the worst

pollution in Europe.
b London is a very good example of this. It has a naturally dense atmosphere, and during the nineteenth and twentieth centuries the use of coal-burning fires and the large number of factories in the area led to an appalling situation. There was so much industrial effluent being dumped into the Thames that, only thirty years ago, anybody who was unlucky enough to fall in the river was immediately rushed to hospital and had their stomach pumped . . .
c This can be seen from the characters in his books . . .

Pointing the way – Study
1f 2b 3a 4e 5c 6d

Pointing the way – Practice
The following are *possible* answers.
1a The only way a country can become genuinely richer is to produce more.
b Indeed, his death made front-page headlines in Italy.
c Nor does increasing wages.
d And yet it can sometimes be a short-term solution.
e . . . it follows that we are in the process of evolving into a new kind of species.
f Nor is it likely that improvements in diet and the reduction of smoking will make the incidence of cancer lower.
g . . . but treatment is improving all the time and it is possible that soon it will be regarded as a comparatively minor complaint.
h Indeed, it is possible that soon it will be regarded as a comparatively minor complaint.
2a If it is true that people refuse to leave their cars at home under any circumstances, all attempts to improve the public transport system are doomed to failure. The only way to relieve traffic congestion is to make traffic lights and junctions work as efficiently as possible.

Unit 20

Using an informal tone – Practice
1a (*possible*) People tell me I shouldn't waste time. Why not? Personally I see the art of doing nothing as a very valuable

⚟ Key to Unit 20

asset. And it happens to be one art I am very good at. If, for example, the urge to do something becomes too strong, I can effectively squash it by making lists of things to do. Mind you, once or twice I have caught myself making lists of the lists I am going to make. This, I admit, is going too far.

Illustrating your statements – Study
2 They could be used to clear him of mass murder.
   They represent the cutting down of trees, which cannot easily be replaced, and therefore should be preserved.
   A coffee tin could be used to start a miniature vegetable garden.
   Somebody worked very hard to make the plastic cup and this effort should be respected.
3a I'll show you a filing problem of DHSS proportions.
 b I resolve to perpetrate a night of the large dustbin bags.
 c Honest toil produced that plastic cup. Am I just going to throw it away? No, I will show my respect . . .
4 It is also difficult to pack chairs and other items of furniture into a suitcase.

Illustrating your statements – Practice
1a (*possible*) Mediterranean Blue sounds nice. It will be like being permanently on holiday. I fall for Egyptian Ochre, with its evocation of the timeless mysteries of the Pharaohs. It is only when I am halfway through transforming the living room that I realize that living in the sea is cold and living entombed in a pyramid is boring.

Notes

Notes